ISBN 978-1-333-32182-6
PIBN 10490016

1 MONTH OF
FREE
READING

at

www.ForgottenBooks.com

By purchasing this book you are eligible for one month membership to ForgottenBooks.com, giving you unlimited access to our entire collection of over 1,000,000 titles via our web site and mobile apps.

To claim your free month visit: www.forgottenbooks.com/free490016

English
Français
Deutsche
Italiano
Español
Português

www.forgottenbooks.com

Mythology Photography **Fiction**
Fishing Christianity **Art** Cooking
Essays Buddhism Freemasonry
Medicine **Biology** Music **Ancient**
Egypt Evolution Carpentry Physics
Dance Geology **Mathematics** Fitness
Shakespeare **Folklore** Yoga Marketing
Confidence Immortality Biographies
Poetry **Psychology** Witchcraft
Electronics Chemistry History **Law**
Accounting **Philosophy** Anthropology
Alchemy Drama Quantum Mechanics
Atheism Sexual Health **Ancient History**
Entrepreneurship Languages Sport
Paleontology Needlework Islam
Metaphysics Investment Archaeology
Parenting Statistics Criminology
Motivational

PREFACE.

NO adequate account of the Draft-riot of 1863 has ever been printed. Contemporary newspaper reports of it were necessarily fragmentary and defective. People at that time residing in New York, including even the men who aided in suppressing the mob, had but an imperfect conception of the magnitude and bloody results of the tumult. The difficulties in the way of obtaining data for a trustworthy record have been very great. The author of this volume has laboriously sifted the press reports for all material contained in them which was worth preserving. He has had access to the telegraph-books of the Police Department, and has carefully examined the hundreds of despatches sent and received during the riot. Many of those have here been quoted in full as a part of the record or illustrating it. Much help has been cheerfully given him by veteran members of the police force and others who were city officials at the time ; by officers of the volunteer and militia forces actively engaged in the struggle with the mob; and by citizens who were eye-witnesses of events narrated. The author himself was then in the city, serving as a volunteer during the first two days of the riot, thereby obtaining vivid impressions which better prepared him for the present work.

The entire mass of material, after collection, has been thoroughly read and criticised by the very highest police authority, and the book as printed contains no statement of fact which has not received the most competent official approval.

The general reader, in order to comprehend the situation, should, from the beginning, bear in mind that the riot took place during the Civil War, in July, 1863, just after the battle of Gettysburg. The entire organized militia of the cities of New York and Brooklyn was absent on duty, having been drawn away by the national government for temporary service in that memorable campaign. Owing to the war, nevertheless, both cities contained large numbers of men who had had experience in the field and were thereby prepared for the emergency.

It is the author's conviction that his toilsome research is fully justified. The present day has its plainly perceptible perils, and with a direct reference to these the great riot offers a number of sufficiently obvious suggestions.

New York, Oct. 1, 1886.

Contents.

Police Precincts marked in Red.

The Elevated Roads, Brooklyn Bridge, etc., left on to show present status, the Police Precincts being the same now as in 1863.

THE VOLCANO

UNDER THE CITY.

I.

The Unexpected Comes.

"Thus far, everything has gone quietly, and the people generally consider the Draft as a matter of course, for we have been unable to learn of any undue excitement in regard to it in any section. Many stories have been circulated to the effect that bands, gangs, and companies have been organized, here and there, with the intention of resisting the Draft, and that the numbers are armed and drilled, hold secret meetings, and so forth; but, from all that we can learn, no such organizations exist; and even if they did, they will amount to nothing."

THAT was the editorial declaration of the *New York Daily Tribune* on Saturday morning, July 11, 1863; and there was no better authority in the country.

Three days later, come to the corner of Broadway and Twenty-third Street. It is the very heart of the city; noon, July 14, 1863.

Where have all the people gone? Why are the streets deserted and the stores closed? Why is the air so full of smoke that you can scarcely breathe? Are those men intoxicated who lie upon the pavement yonder? What is this awful crash and rattle which seems to come from every direction?

Stand still for a few minutes and look and listen.

That which all men said could not and would not come has come. The mob has risen, and the greatest riot known in American history is at its height.

It is an affair intensely interesting and well worthy of careful study. At this hour, a Volunteer Special, begrimed with two days of hot-weather service, is sufficiently rough-looking to be almost safe, even here on Broadway, but no carefully dressed person would be so. Scores of men have been beaten half to death for the offence of wearing good clothes. It is a terrible time for women and children. Business is dead. The ships at the wharves have ceased loading or unloading. All the street-car lines have been compelled to stop running. Nearly all the telegraph-lines are down. The police are apparently beaten.

The militia regiments are all in Pennsylvania. The people are rallying fast to suppress the tumult and are organizing, but in the mean time the work of destruction goes on. The mob have kindled twenty-four fires since yesterday morning, and some of these have burned whole blocks of buildings. The rioters have plundered houses and shops and stores, murdered men, maltreated women, destroyed an orphan asylum, and now threaten to do more and worse.

The men upon the pavement yonder are not drunk; they are dead. They will be buried in due season, but you and I will never know how or by whom. The coroners have ceased holding inquests. The Burial Permit Bureau is not in operation. The cemeteries cannot be reached, from many parts of the city. There will never be any public record of the death of those men, but the real cause in each case is worth examining into, for the apparent cause was evidently the club of a policeman.

As we stand here, there is a crowd coming up Broadway, and they must be looked at as they pass.

They are whooping, yelling, blaspheming, howling, demoniac, such as no man imagined the city of New York to contain. There are women among them, and boys half grown, but none of them seem to be Americans. Who are they?

That is a very important question, and can be answered only after a more searching inquiry than can be made off-hand. Changing the form into "What are they?" this look at them partly answers it.

They carry guns, pistols, axes, hatchets, crow-bars, pitchforks, knives, bludgeons, — the Red Flag. Much of their shouting is done in other tongues, but that cry is in English: "Down with the rich men! Down with property! Down with the police!"

It is an insurrection of evil against law; an up-rising of suppressed hellish forces against order. They mean precisely what they shout, and are fiercely carrying into effect their declared pur-poses.

Could this bursting-forth have been prevented?

Decidedly it could have been, if our law-abid-ing, self-confident public could have believed be-forehand that such a thing as this was possible. The crust over this volcano broke through at the want-of-preparation point, and all the other crust gave way. As for the crowd here, it is much like the others which, as a Volunteer Special, I have taken note of. Those fellows in front are all ex-convicts, of one crime or another. There is hardly an American among them, even by adoption, still less by birth. A German, Irishman, Frenchman, any other man, coming here and really becoming American will keep out of such business. Those men have not ceased to be foreigners at heart, and have brought with them and kept in them all their inheritance of bitterness and brutality. As for any specific object in this present outbreak, they have none. They have not thought so far as that.

The army in the field needed men ; the President ordered a conscription, under the law ; the incidents of the enforcement of the conscription provided an occasion ; the under-world seized the opportunity and broke loose, for a few hours calling itself a " Draft-riot." It is easy, now, to discover its real character. Just such a volcano is continually in a state of perfect preparation in this and every other large city, and in many smaller gatherings of the required elements of disorder. The forces increase rather than diminish, and the ready peril asks for less and less in the way of an apparent excuse or palliation.

The writer of this book considers himself on duty, now as in July, 1863, as a Volunteer Special, with a very possible riot slumbering near him.

In telling the plain story of a fierce, midsummer madness which once came to the city of New York, the use proposed is somewhat more than the relation of an interesting episode. The signs of the times are such as summon thoughtful men to put away the indifference and unbelief which then held open wide the gate through which disaster poured in. Most important of all thoughtful men, and most directly spoken to, are the thoughtful working-men whose hands hold the entire political power of this country. They are well aware of the futility and absurdity of crime as a means or method in political operations. Outside of them, around them, controllable by them, is a vast mass of ignorance, recklessness, and depravity which does not think. To this mass, life itself seems a failure. It broods and sulks and suffers and has no hope, and it could not break loose without doing harm, unmixed with good of any sort.

The hands of American labor hold the ballot and do not need to take up the dynamite cartridge or the torch or the carbine. The American

laborer has no excuse for following blind, imported guides into ditches of blood and fire.

The history of all madness teaches that it will
do, in its frenzied paroxysms, what every-day
sanity has no dream of doing. History also
records in many repetitions the unaccountable
suddenness with which masses of men will take
the infection of a great craze.

The country as a whole has forgotten that
there was ever a really great riot in the city of
New York. Its own population is better aware
that there was a serious disturbance connected,
in some vague manner, with the " Draft" during
the Civil War. Yet very few even of those who,
like the writer of this book, were present, seeing
in part and hearing in part, have any clear idea of
the extent and nature of the terrible event.

There was a great riot, and it was only in small
part either political or sectarian. What it really
was must be shown step by step. The volcanic
forces which broke loose had no apparent sufficient cause for such an eruption. They had no
attainable object. They were under no known
leadership or direction. They had but a slight
and crude prior organization. Nevertheless they
did an appalling amount of mischief.

There have been, and in other lands there yet may be, such things as righteous revolutions, accompanied by tumultuous uprisings of suppressed social elements. There cannot be any need for tumult, violence, bloodshed, and devastation in these free United States, where the individual man, the voter, is ruler. It must, therefore, be accepted as an axiom that a mob of violence in the United States is a mob of crime. It is composed of criminal units, in the act of committing felony, who must be dealt with accordingly. The best dealing is the shortest, and begins at the beginning.

A mere outbreak may occur in one of many unexpected ways, but the core of any great sedition must consist, even at the outset, of men and women who have previously been guilty of criminal acts or are morally prepared for such commission. What a flood may sweep with it, once it is well a-going, will appear with sufficient plainness from the following record.

Such a nucleus, the first requisite of a mob, was found in 1863. It exists now, ready for action, in hundreds of localities, and the friends of labor and of law must watch it.

The second requisite for a great riot is the existence of real or supposed grievances, bitter enough to give force and effect to a rallying-cry. Such grievances, both real and imaginary, now everywhere exist in the disturbed relations between labor and capital. The daily crime of permitting these allies to be enemies marks the low and heathenish standard of what is called statesmanship.

A third requisite before crime will be ready to lead a tumult is a supposed or actual weakness of the known repressive forces. This, in New York, in 1863, was provided by the absence of nearly all the organized militia regiments, in response to a military necessity of the nation.

A fourth indispensable condition is a heated, feverish state of the social elements capable of rioting. The fuel must be ready to kindle. How this preparation was then made will be shown. Everything is very ready indeed at the present time, and will continue to be so until a change comes.

A fifth and highly important condition is the habitual refusal of sober-minded people to believe that there is any volcano.

The quotation from the *New York Daily Tribune*, at the beginning of this chapter, is selected from many like utterances to illustrate the accepted view of the situation in 1863. The press reporters discovered very little fever; the police did not see any signs of danger; the authorities were very sure there was no "crater." Only through the deceptive crust of a false security could there have been such a ruinous bursting-up.

All who thus studied and denied erred as to the nature of the possible peril to be watched against, for they were entirely correct in declaring that the state of the popular mind with reference to the Draft was by no means seriously threatening. It was in the middle of the third year of the Civil War. The United States Government had been compelled to follow the lead of the Confederates and resort to conscription instead of volunteering in order to supply its armies. Men opposed to the war itself, to the Lincoln Administration, and the merely seditious, had made all the political capital possible out of the fact and the methods of the conscription; yet the result of their efforts was well stated by the *Tribune,* and by other journals that used similar language. The specific features of the conscription or "draft" will be presented in their proper place.

The War Department had published its formal announcement that the enrolment was complete, and that the draft would begin on the 11th of July. So strong was official faith in the existing order of things that no further notification was sent to the Mayor or to the Board of Metropolitan Police. No requisition was made for a police guard to preserve order at the several enrolment offices at which the Draft was to take place. No unusual military force was provided. The only shadow of such a precaution was the fact that a regiment of the Invalid Corps (crippled soldiers, five hundred strong,—or, rather, five hundred weak) was directed to furnish proper guard details. On Saturday morning, July 11th, and on Monday morning, July 13th, such details were duly made, but they were regarded as mere matters of form and ceremony — something like regulation "guard-mounting" in time of peace. The brave but helpless fellows furnished a mere picture and suggestion of the armed force actually demanded by the facts of the situation.

It was generally well known that the Governor of the State, Hon. Horatio Seymour, had been and still was in correspondence with the national government, with a view to a prevention, mitiga·

tion, or postponement of the Draft, and there were many who believed that he would succeed or had succeeded.   His efforts were without result, except that the fact of their making was one element of the general suspense.   He was an acute and experienced political observer, yet it does not appear that he, more than others, was in any fear of extended disorder.

In spite of all the seeming quiet, nevertheless, there were—increasingly at the very last—dark rumors of trouble to come.   They circulated whisperingly from house to house through all the lower wards of the city.   There were, moreover, some clear-headed citizens who began to not only perceive the presence of possible danger but to also prepare to meet it.   It is a curious feature of the situation that not the timid men or the noncombatants, but some of the military officers who for various reasons remained in the city were fairly well awakened to the impending crisis before it aroused the suspicions of those who were supposed to be professionally on the watch for its indications.   There were mutual conferences and exchanges of opinion among these gentlemen, of which there is no exact record, and small informal gatherings of them, in more places than one, to discuss the situation, were held on Sunday, the 12th of July.

It was merely by a sort of professional instinct that, on Saturday, Police Superintendent Kennedy made a detail of a sergeant and fifteen policemen to take charge of the Arsenal at Thirty-fifth Street and Seventh Avenue, and to hold it until relieved by a suitable military guard. No authority asked for them, nobody knew precisely why they were sent, and they could not long have held their vitally important post against any considerable party of assailants. They were an indication of vague and undefinable uneasiness, and that was all. There were many muskets and much ammunition in the Arsenal, however, and the police guard may have been sent there in time to prevent a world of mischief.

On Saturday morning, the 11th of July, 1863, the actual operation of the Draft began, at the Marshal's or Enrolment Office of the Third Subdivision of the Ninth Congressional District, at No. 677 Third Avenue, corner of Forty-sixth Street. The drawings of names were made by means of a lottery-wheel, and proceeded throughout the day without any interruption whatever,

The crowd assembled was large and contained many cloudy faces, but all utterances of discontent were seemingly within the bounds of reason. The leaders of the coming riot seem to have required the results of that day's work in order to bring their recklessness up to the proper point; or it may be that such plans as they had formed included the precise date, the 13th, fixed upon for the general Draft, all over the city. Twelve hundred and thirty-six names were drawn, leaving only 264 men to be obtained in order to complete the quota of that subdivision. No other enrolment office was ready or attempted a beginning of operations that day. When the lottery-wheel ceased its intensely-watched revolutions, the crowd slowly dispersed. The drafted men had yet some days left in which to arrange their affairs and report for duty, or the reverse, but they all went away more or less gloomily. In proportion to the measure of their patriotism or war-spirit, or the pressure of their circumstances, or their mental and moral condition, the oppressive nature of the Conscription Act became manifest to them. Its tremendous reality also dawned upon them and upon the entire community. It was a fact, and one from which no manner of escape was provided for any drafted man who could not raise three hundred dollars to pay his exemption-fee or furnish a substitute. There was no question raised by anybody as to the fairness and impartiality of the day's work at the marshal's office. The 1236 names were distributed among all classes, ranks, and conditions, and the laborer and the millionaire were alike before the even-handed law. As to the " mob element," it was well understood that a larger proportion of this than of any other had escaped enrolment, owing to its drifting, uncertain residence and the extreme difficulty experienced by the enrolling officers in specifying its individual members. No property-owner and no man in regular business could escape the search; but the vagrant, the unknown, the men accustomed to conceal their whereabouts, avoided the hated " wheel " by the thousand.

In spite of this fact, however, a number of names were drawn that day of men whose previous course of life had made them well known to the police, and doubts were freely expressed by the latter as to whether all of these would actually take their places in the ranks of the army.

It may have been just as well for the army that many of the worst of them unintentionally elected to be mowed down by grape and canister in the streets of New York. Such difficulty as the police thus anticipated was with desperate men as individuals and not in any organized or collective capacity.

The purely political opponents of the conscription of men for the armies of the United States had been in a manner deprived of strength by the recent victories at Gettysburg and Vicksburg, and were disposed to quiet. No anti-administration leader of any social standing or name or influence was or could be an advocate of anarchy. An entirely different element was nearly ready to avail itself of the situation.

The next day, the 12th of July, was Sunday. It was passed in a sort of suppressed fermentation by nearly the entire population. The coolest although most deeply interested men were the Metropolitan Police, who were hardly affected by the growing excitement. The external signs of its effect upon others escaped them altogether, or, if observed, were regarded as indicating nothing of importance. All the discussions of the evil to come, and there must have been many

such, were held in secret places; but their existence seemed to send out an atmosphere of its
own that brooded heavily over the whole city.
Quiet citizens in their houses felt that there was
trouble in the air, and wondered what it might
be. There were fires in two or three places on
Sunday evening, but nobody connected them
with the Draft, and it was only noticed that they
seemed to attract larger and more disorderly
crowds than ordinarily.

The fact already alluded to, that this atmosphere pervaded and affected the several informal
coteries of militia and volunteer officers, afterwards became of great importance. These gentlemen discussed the subject of a possible riot
as a military problem, and took into professional
consideration what might best be done by themselves in case of such an emergency. As a con-
sequence, they were better prepared for prompt
and effective action during the next twenty-four
hours. On the whole, Sunday passed so quietly
that its close presented no feature which seemed
to call for especial action by either the civil or
military authorities.

There were many reasons why the police were
entirely justified in their calm assurance of se-

curity. They had good ground for their confidence in their own ability to deal with any possible disorder in the city of New York. The State and the National governments were in like manner justifiable.

It remains unquestionably true, nevertheless, that the one factor of safety which was entirely absent was a vital one : if the danger had been seen and acknowledged, it would have been provided for, and there would have been no riot extending beyond the street and square upon which it began.

II.

The Black Joke.

ON Sunday evening, July 12th, no more than
the customary details for duty were made
by the Superintendent of Metropolitan Police.
He had at his disposal about a thousand men,'
well trained and entirely trustworthy, being that
half of the entire force which was " on duty."
The other half was " off duty," for its daily rest,
but subject to summons, constituting it an available reserve. The thousand or more men on duty
were scattered all over the city. The station-
house of each of the thirty-two precincts * was the
local headquarters and rallying-point of the men
belonging to that precinct. Each station-house
was connected by telegraph with the Central
Office, the general business of the department
being transacted through the wires. All messages of any importance were duly recorded, in
ordinary times. That part of the force intrusted

---

* For the location of each of these, see *Appendix*, page 336;
also *Map* of the city.

with the care of the city of Brooklyn, across the East River but included in the Metropolitan Police District, was similarly circumstanced.

The Board of Metropolitan Police was invested with the power of calling out and employing the militia regiments within its jurisdiction, but these all, seventeen in number, were now out of reach.

Superintendent Kennedy had no thought of needing militia regiments or of any special pressure upon what seemed the ample force under his direction. It was purely as a routine precaution that he ordered a sergeant and twelve men to proceed to each of the United States enrolment offices on Monday morning. It was well understood that crowds of men would then be gathered at those places, and it was a regular duty of the police to be present wherever a crowd might assemble.

The proposed preservation of the public peace was the only requisition in the case, and it was believed that the squads of Metropolitans detailed would be sufficient to insure that.

The United States officer in command of the regiment of the Invalid Corps, Colonel Ruggles, formerly of General Pope's staff, made his regulation "details," but they were late in starting to their posts of duty, and were much too late in arriving. Very little more was heard of them during the riots, although they served as garrisons of posts, here and there. They had done their best service on other fields, and were poorly adapted to the rough-and-tumble struggle of putting down a mob.

The mayor of the city, Hon. George Opdyke, came to his office at an early hour, for word had reached him that there might be disturbances in the course of the day. A friendly warning had also been sent him that his own residence might be assailed, but he quietly and bravely disregarded it. He was partly right, for none of the anti-war political leaders of whom he had any personal knowledge proposed to hurt either him or his family or his dwelling, however much they might regret the political fact that he was mayor of New York. It was well for his property, however, if not for its human inmates, that some of his neighbors learned of the giving of the warning and took a different view of the matter. The house had an armed guard before it (and not by the mayor's orders), just about in season.

The nominal, and officially the actual, commander of the militia of the metropolis was

Major-General Charles Sandford, a brave old officer, to whom it was almost in vain to carry any startling or menacing report or rumor. He was one of the last to believe that there was or could be any real danger brewing; and even after the riot was in full blast, and his own men, directed by his more wide-awake subordinates, were firing volleys down street after street, it was almost impossible to make him comprehend the gravity of the situation. He persisted in sending telegrams to Police Headquarters that "all is quiet," during the very hours of Monday when Police-President Acton's force was struggling for life against overwhelming numbers, and again towards the close of the week, when yet the mob held almost undisputed possession of entire wards.

The commander of the United States Military District which included New York was Major-General John E. Wool, an army officer distinguished in three wars, but whose age and infirmities unfitted him to deal with circumstances so new to him and so surprisingly trying and perplexing. He could much better have directed an organized army in the field of battle than have handled miscellaneous forces of all sorts in a hurly-burly street fight of several days' duration. He was quickly compelled to abandon all idea of personally supervising or directing any part of them. The immediate command of the United States troops in and about the port of New York devolved upon Brigadier-General Harvey Brown, of the United States Regular Army. He also was a veteran of many battle-fields, and he proved to be by no means out of place in this one. On being summoned to the scene of action, with a quick shrewdness and a putting aside of all mere "service" prejudices which did him honor, he at once proceeded to the Police Head-quarters in Mulberry Street, and there remained, not only as commanding and directing his own men, but also as the unflinching, unhesitating counsellor and ally of Mr. Acton, the President of the Board of Police Commissioners.

It had been ordered that all the enrolment offices should be ready for proceeding with the Draft, and it was not doubted but that they would duly begin their work on Monday morning. They were not quite ready, however, and the greater part of them were yet busy with their final preparations during the morning hours. Before noon all the marshals had received further orders to cease work and convey the con-

tents of their offices to places of greater security.

There were men who proposed to act as leaders in whatever were to be the extraordinary
events of the day. At a very early hour they
and their emissaries pervaded the city in all directions, carrying the word that the time for
active opposition to the Draft had come. They
went to every point where there was work to be
done that day which would assemble laboring
men, to notify them that they must not go on
with their toil, on penalty of violence. The
wharves were visited, the foundries, machine-
shops, ship-yards, factories, printing-houses, and
similar haunts of industry, and all the workmen
there, and all gangs of laborers upon public works,
were summoned to join the ranks of the anti-
Draft demonstration. As far north as the great
Croton Reservoir in Central Park, the engineer in
charge found himself compelled to begin operations with only half his force of men. Some
went home in fear, but more went down-town to
see what might be going on. As a rule, all that
was asked for by the "working-men" thus notified was proper protection from mob violence,
and not a solitary establishment was disabled by

the absence of its "skilled labor." Yet, as for honest laboring men, of all political parties, thousands of them were entirely willing to parade the streets in an "anti-Draft demonstration," and to do any required amount of shouting and all that sort of thing, who were at the same time not at all inclined to commit either burglary or arson or murder.

The line between violent felony and anything bearing a shadow of political purpose or acccomplishment was soon to be drawn with startling distinctness. The later recruiting processes of the mob were a pure terrorism. There is nothing else so brutally tyrannical as Crime enforcing a miscellaneous "conscription" on its own account. Squads of half-drunken wretches then marched hither and thither, forcing honest men to quit the toil by which they earned their bread. As many as could not escape, or were at all half-willing to "go on a spree," were compelled to swell the ranks of the rioters and march along with them. They dragged on in this manner many an ordinarily peaceable fellow to a drunken orgie stained with crime after crime, and to a dog's burial in the Potter's Field.

Before 9 o'clock A.M. a great deal of recruiting had been done, in various parts of the city, but, as yet, not at any point save one had there been made a gathering whose size or apparent purposes were such as to arouse alarm or call for special action by the authorities. It was a matter of course that there should be large and increasing crowds in the neighborhoods of the several enrolment offices. All men whose names had been enrolled were naturally expected to be on hand to learn their individual fates, and, so long as they should behave themselves, their right so to do was unquestionable. It was not, therefoie, with any anticipation of serious trouble to come that the deputy provost-marshal in charge of the enrolment office at the corner of Third Avenue and Forty-sixth Street saw the approaches to it thronged with gloomy-faced men when he and his assistants proceeded to their post of duty. Once they were inside of the building, the very density of the mass which gathered and grew around the half-guarded doorway prevented any clear idea or correct information coming through it as to the deeds performing or preparing in the outer world.

At the same hour a modified copy of the state of things on Third Avenue began to assume form around the enrolment office at No. 1084½ Broadway, for the Eighth Congressional District, composed of the Eighteenth, Twentieth, and Twenty-first wards of the city; but the crowd there was not so large, its readiness for mischief was not so complete, and the storm did not burst there until a later hour of the day.

Work began at the Third Avenue office at the usual hour, but there were many preliminaries before the wheel could be set in motion. There was a police sergeant on duty, with about a dozen men, but the Invalid Corps detail had not arrived. At about nine o'clock the street-cars were compelled to stop running on both Second and Third avenues, at and above Sixty-sixth Street, and their drivers were notified not to attempt further trips. At the same time a number of men began to cut down the telegraph-poles and sunder the wires near the enrolment office, with the evident idea of interrupting the communications of the city authorities. This was the first overt act of the mob, and it should be borne in mind as plainly indicating previous planning and forethought. It was not the outbreak of any sudden burst of passion, and it contemplated something more than an attack upon that particular enrolment office.

3

The crowd itself was not by any means made up from the immediate neighborhood, which, however, contained a full proportion of rough and lawless characters. All the drinking-houses in the vicinity were doing an uncommonly lively business.

Before nine o'clock so many telegraph-poles were down that the rioters considered that part of their work done; but their object was defeated by the courage and coolness of one man. Mr. James Crowley, Superintendent of the Police Telegraph System, was on his way down from his residence to the Police Central Office. He was entirely unsuspicious of any disturbance until attracted by the crowd and the noise. He at once comprehended the situation. The fallen wires lay in the gutter at the street side, and he knew that the police special wires were among them. He gathered all, as they came to hand, wound them around a lamp-post and "grounded" them so as to secure operation. He was, of course, interrupted by threats of violence and by profane demands as to the meaning of it, but he coolly replied that he was "Only getting the wires out of your way, boys." He was therefore not murdered on the spot, as he surely would have been if the nature of his performance and the fact of his connection with the Police had been discovered. The Central Office thereby retained some of its most important up-town connections until a later hour of the riotings. Immediately after his daring feat, Mr. Crowley hastened to the Twenty-first Precinct Police Station, on Thirty-fifth Street, and telegraphed the facts of the case to the Central Office. This is supposed to be the first trustworthy intimation of the real nature of the trouble that was received there.

Word was brought to the police station-house in East Fifty-ninth Street of the threatening aspect of affairs, and Captain G. T. Porter, commanding the precinct, set out at once, with such men as he could muster, to reinforce the squad already on duty at the Third Avenue enrolment office. He stationed most of his men, about sixty all told, inside of the building, and awaited results, but with little idea of an assault too powerful to be resisted by sixty Metropolitans.

Enough was previously known at the Central Office to indicate a necessity of preparing for something more than common, and the following general order was sent out by telegraph at 9 o'clock A.M.:

" To all Stations in New York and Brooklyn : Call in your reserves. Platoon and hold them at the station-house subject to further orders.   J. A. KENNEDY."

Not long after sending this despatch, Superintendent Kennedy set out in person to visit the scene of the possible disturbance, and to attend to other parts of his customary routine. So little did he know of the matter, however, and so faintly did he imagine the bitter passions with which he was to deal, that he went alone, in a buggy. He went first to the Thirty-fifth Street Arsenal, and then drove to a point some distance below the enrolment office, where he left his buggy in charge of its driver and proceeded on foot. He was not a United States Government officer, and was not at all concerned in the enforcement of the Draft. Why should he have any cause to fear ? His peril lay deeper than that, for he was the head and front of all lawful repression of crime and restraint of criminals. The instant he was recognized he was assailed with shouts and execrations, knocked down and terribly beaten. He was a strong man, of iron courage, and he struggled desperately for his life. Knocked down again and again and mercilessly beaten, he as often regained his feet and fled, pursued by his savage assailants. These had no visible reasons whatever for murdering him, but seemed utterly bent upon doing so. Covered with mud and blood, he was almost un-recognizable, but saw among the men who came running to the place of his last assault one good citizen whom he knew.

" John Egan," he shouted, " save my life!"

A quick and vigorous response resulted in a rescue, and the Superintendent of Police was carried to the Central Office on a dray. He arrived just as Mr. Acton, the President of the Police Board, was coming out ; and the latter, yet uninformed of the circumstances, and not guessing the personality of the battered and apparently drunken form on the dray, said to an attendant officer,

"Lock him up! Lock him up!"

Mr. Kennedy was not locked up, but remained under the surgeon's care, in a critical condition, until many days after the riots had been put down.

There had been one gathering on Sunday evening which was not, so far as can be ascertained, in communication or relation with any other, and yet which was productive of terrible consequences. It formed no part of any general plan or plot, and

had no thought of a general sedition. Its deci-
sions and its subsequent action point a peculiar
lesson of special interest.

Fire Engine Company Number Thirty-three
was composed exclusively of the class of men
known as " roughs," and they are not necessarily
criminals by any means. They were the free-
handed, daring, turbulent, volunteer firemen of
the old time, eagerly ready at any hour for what
they called a " muss." Their engine was popular-
ly known as the " Black Joke," and their engine-
house was on Fifty-eighth Street, near Broadway,
at some distance from the Third Avenue enrol·
ment office. Their leading rough had been drawn
in the conscription on Saturday, with a few others,
and all the " boys" decided that the proper thing
to do, under such circumstances, was to smash
the enrolment office, break the wheel, burn the
papers, and so destroy any evidence that the Draft
had called for their man. These were the men
who headed the first charge made, and it is believed that they did it without any consideration
of what was to follow.

Of all these things the busy officials inside of
the enrolment office had but a very imperfect
and illusory information. They were brave men,

steadily intent upon the performance of their sworn duty. At last the hated lottery-of-life wheel began its revolutions, and by half-past ten o'clock about seventy-five names had been drawn.

Before leaving the Central Office, Superintendent Kennedy had ordered reinforcing squads of policemen to be sent to the several enrolment offices, and he had been gone but a quarter of an hour before this telegram was received from the Nineteenth Precinct station-house, in Fifty-ninth Street:

"The laborers have all suspended work, and are gathering with crowbars and other missiles in different parts of this and the Twenty-second Precinct, to make a grand demonstration at 677 Third Avenue."

The "demonstration" had been prepared a great deal earlier than that, however, and it was not to be made by gangs of striking laborers scattered over two city wards.

Sixty policemen preserved a fair semblance of good order within and around the doors of the Third Avenue enrolment office until the arrival of an appointed hour. No doubt the "Black Joke" roughs affiliated rudely with such other elements of mischief as they found assembled on the avenue. They were not the kind of men to proceed more slowly because of such an unlooked-for mass of miscellaneous support. Fire Company Thirty-three was bound to smash that wheel, and there were more "cops" on duty than had been by any means expected; so the more help the better.

At thirty minutes past ten o'clock somebody fired a pistol-shot in the street, in front of the fated building. Instantly, as if a signal agreed upon had been given, a storm of stones broke in the windows of the enrolment office. This was followed by the determined rush of a strong and compact body of men,—the "Black Joke" roughs, followed by some hundreds of others,—and the great riot of 1863 had begun.

From that moment the mob of New York City was let loose. Its different elements burst out and operated according to their several natures. A part continued to imagine itself acting in opposition to the conscription law, and much of this part went home early, refusing a share in the work of the remainder. By far the greater part of that remainder cared only for the simple fact that the barriers of lawful authority seemed to be temporarily swept away. The fever which is common to all occasions of popular excitement began to rage in the blood of the unruly, the violent, the depraved.

Men who were devoid of moral or mental self-control believed themselves set free from any other repression, and excitement and strong drink brought out their inner natures.

Captain Porter and his sixty policemen stood their ground heroically against the overwhelming rush of the rioters, using no fire-arms for fear of hurting innocent men, and succeeded in giving the Draft officials time to escape with their lives through the rear of the building. They even carried off the "wheel" and many papers and records with them. Then, after a desperate charge and a hand-to-hand struggle, the Metropolitans made good their own escape into the open air, with many bruises, but without the loss of a man.

At about the same time, or a few minutes earlier, there came marching up the avenue a company of the Invalid Corps, detailed to act as a nominal "guard." It numbered about fifty men, and was almost instantly swallowed up by the surging masses of the mob. A shower of paving-stones and other missiles came hurtling in among the astonished ranks, and the men began to go down. The officer in command, utterly bewildered by so sudden and unlooked-for an attack, ordered the volleys of stones to be replied to by a volley of blank cartridges, which did but empty the rifles of half his men and leave them defenceless. In utter desperation and without orders, according to some reports, one rank fired with ball, and several of the attacking rioters were killed or wounded. No chance was given for reloading or for further struggling.

The thronging mob broke up the feeble lines and wrenched the useless weapons from almost unresisting hands. A scene of furious brutality followed, the rioters seeming to feel that they were justified in all extremities of cruelty towards mere soldiers who had dared to " fire upon the people," as some of their apologists afterwards phrased the matter.

The greater part of the Invalids managed to escape with nothing worse than a terrific beating, but two of them were pounded to death on the spot. A third was pursued towards the river to a ledge of rocks, to which he fled for safety, and was hurled down from them. The stones and boulders cast upon him soon hid his battered corpse from sight, and the New York mob had set its seal upon its own character. It seems a pity that its first victims should have been a lot of crippled soldier-boys whose only crime, at the uttermost, was that they dared to do some‑ thing in defence of their lives.

The " Black Joke " firemen had entirely failed in their express errand, but the general mob in and about the enrolment office had not gathered with special reference to the Draft-papers and the wheel. They had other work on hand, and a great deal of it. The office itself was sacked in a moment of time, and was at once set on fire. The upper stories of the building were occupied as a tenement-house by several families of the poorer class. Wives and children of working-men were barely permitted to escape with their lives before their homes were in a blaze. They were not allowed to rescue their household goods. At a little after eleven o'clock, that morning, Captain Porter sent to the Central Office this mournful memorandum :

"The marshal's office on Third Avenue is burning down. The police is of no avail.'

It was even so. The fire-alarm was sounded,

as usual, and the nearest fire companies were promptly on the ground, but the mob-leaders sternly forbade their doing anything towards putting out the fire.

These companies were all organized upon the old "volunteer" system, and some of their membership, like the men of Company No. 33, seemed to be half-way in sympathy with the nominal opponents of the Draft. Such conduct at this and other points during the riots had a direct and powerful influence upon the subsequent abolition of their entire organization and the substitution of the existing "paid" department.

A sufficient number of the firemen remained faithful, however, and would have done their duty but for forcible opposition. A fellow named Andrews, a Virginian, took the opportunity of making an insurrectionary speech to the crowd while the building was burning. He was not an agent of the Confederate Government. Subsequent developments proved him a very low person indeed.

The building was fired in several places and burned down rapidly. Away down the avenue, the reinforced police were struggling back towards the spot and sending to the Central Office appeals for additional help, but they could not get within two or three blocks of the fire. It was not until twenty-five minutes past twelve o'clock that Chief Engineer John Decker, of the Fire Department, could obtain an opportunity to address the crowd. A press reporter lurking among them managed to take down the simple plea of the brave fireman, and it contains several points which make it worthy of lasting record :

" FELLOW-CITIZENS : I stand here before you to appeal to your common-sense. I will not say a word at present as to the rights of your cause. About the Draft you doubtless feel you are right. There is no mistake, it is a hard thing for a man to have to leave his home and go soldiering if he did not wish to go ; but I can't argue that question now. You probably feel that you are right in what you have done. You came here to do a certain thing. You have done it. Now you ought to be satisfied. All the United States property is destroyed, and I now appeal to your common-sense to let us, as firemen, go to work and save the property of innocent men. The men whose houses are now burning are innocent. They have nothing to do with the Draft. They know nothing of it. They are hard-working men like yourselves. Now I ask you, will you let us go to work and put out this fire?"

The very worst of the destroyers of the marshal's office had already departed to other deeds of a similar character. The remaining throng answered the Chief Engineer with a round of cheers, and he and his men were permitted to begin their attempt, for several adjoining buildings were burning fast. It is quite likely that the cheering was started by some of the bolder of the immediate neighbors, but John Decker made his speech at the imminent peril of being beaten to death on the spot. He at once got his engines into position, but before they could throw a drop of water on the fire the departing rear-guard of the actual "mob" heard of what he was intending and came howling back. In less than a minute they cleared the avenue of all who resisted them, drove the firemen away from their engines, and stoned the police out of the neighborhood. They took temporary possession of the engines and hose-carts, but, for some unreason, did no injury to the machinery. They soon, however, wearied of so empty a triumph, and went off to other mischief. As soon as they were gone, Decker again got possession of his engines. The delay had been of little more than half an hour's duration, but it had given the flames a tremendous advantage. He, managed to save a part of the building on the corner of Forty-seventh Street, but all the rest of the block was utterly destroyed.

The newspaper reporters present at the beginning of the Third Avenue affair, and they were men every way competent to form a sound opinion, declared that in this mob there was a plainly discernible and pretty well organized nucleus of about three hundred men, under some kind of organization and leadership. This at first might have been the "Black Joke" firemen, but not after their rush had been completed. Precisely such a nucleus became a noticeable feature elsewhere and afterwards. It was sure to present a strong rear-guard, and it directed and led the movements of the general crowds from place to place. It seemed even to have definite purposes, not altogether insane, in some instances.

During the twenty-four hours following this first incendiarism there were twenty-four distinct "fires" reported in different parts of the city, all kindled by the rioters, and all eventually paid for by the working-men of the city of New York. There cannot be any tax levied and collected which does not at the last come upon them in one form and manner or another. They, of all men, are under bonds to be the enemies of every kind of waste, whether it be done by the hands of a mob or by mere political corruption.

III.

Burned Alive.

THE news of this black beginning of the riot spread fast and far, but not many men were prepared to believe that the trouble would be more than local and confined to the destruction of Draft enrolment machinery. The Mayor of New York had already summoned a special meeting of the Board of Aldermen to discuss measures for the preservation of the peace of the city, and was in consultation with the military commanders, State and National. Telegrams were flashing out in swift succession from the Central Office of the Metropolitan Police, calling in all outlying details of men, and making other preparations for a desperate struggle. Still, it was no time for giving explanations, and as late as 11.30 A.M. the down-town station-houses sent up telegrams inquiring, " Is there a riot up-town?"

The " reserves," or off-duty men, of eleven pre-

cincts were ordered to the scene of action on
Third Avenue as fast as possible before noon, but
could not be gathered and sent in sufficient force
to be of any greater use than that of holding a
part of their enemies temporaily in check.

The mob was rising in other parts of the city,
and wherever any considerable number of its ruffians came together they seemed to consider it
their first duty to find and pursue and beat to
death some helpless colored man.

The work of the Draft was but just beginning
at the other enrolment offices when, at 11.25
o'clock A.M., they received telegraphic orders to
suspend. The Sixth Avenue deputy marshal
was even ordered to carry his books and papers
to Governor's Island for safety. It was well and
generally understood that there would be no
more draft that day, and that all its machinery
was speedily beyond reach of any such undertaking as that of the " Black Joke" firemen. By
noon of Monday, therefore, the operations of the
conscription law had been reasonably disconnected from all the buildings in which they had
been carried on. The Draft itself had been forcibly suspended, and there was practically nothing more to be done in that direction. The po-

lice and what there was of the military had been overpowered, however, for the first time in the history of the city, and the mob experienced, through all its fast-heating veins, a sudden sense of power. It would not, could not stop. It would go on and obtain control of the city. It would work its will with property and with the limbs and lives of all against whom it had any prejudice or hatred. It would say little or nothing more about the Draft,—the politicians and the newspapers might have that for themselves,—but it would sack, burn, torture, and murder until its real character should be satisfactorily expressed.

The Central Office at an early hour sent out a general despatch of " No drill to-day," that there might be no useless fatigue of men who were likely soon to have all they could endure. At ten minutes past twelve the first despatch relating to Superintendent Kennedy's injury arrived, so complete had been the confusion among the up-town precincts, and so little had been known among them of the actual events of the morning. The very police engaged in the prolonged struggle on Third Avenue, as late as 12.35 o'clock sent in telegrams saying, " Tell the Superintendent we would like to have some help." There was none to be sent as yet; but President Acton was now aware that the burden of responsibility had fallen upon his shoulders, and he had taken it up.

The police force on Third Avenue was losing ground in spite of unsurpassed heroism. They were not using fire-arms as yet, but were plying their clubs more and more mercilessly, for the mob gathered behind them as well as before, and they were practically "at bay." At a quarter past twelve o'clock a telegram came to the Central Office:

"There is danger of the mob attacking the Armory corner of Twenty-first Street and Second Avenue. There is about five hundred stand of arms in it."

Fifteen minutes later a similar message concluded with: "There is a great crowd. One of our men has—" And there it stopped, for there were many broken and disjointed messages in that hour of difficulty.

The armory building alluded to, on the northeastern corner of Second Avenue and Twenty-first Street, was a large brick structure built for a piano-factory, but now occupied as a rifle-factory, the entire upper story being used as a drill-room by military organizations. The quantity of arms stored there was probably about as stated, but a much larger quantity was known to be in the Union Steam Works building, one block above, on the corner of Second Avenue and Twenty-second Street. The latter building was largely occupied for the manufacture of carbines for army uses. There was also supposed to be a small quantity of ammunition in each; and the plans of the mob evidently included obtaining so desirable a supply of weapons.

Captain Cameron, of the Eighteenth Precinct, had already acted promptly with reference to the Armory. The section of police commonly known as the "Broadway Squad," and composed of picked men, had been sent to him, thirty-two strong, under Sergeant Burdick. They reported to him at noon, and were at once ordered to proceed to the Armory and hold it at all hazards until relief could be sent them. No steps could at that moment be taken with reference to the Union Steam Works, and they did not seem to be threatened. The mob may not yet have known that they contained over four thousand carbines and rifle-muskets. The Broadway Squad reached their post of peril singly and in pairs, slipping in as best they could. The mob surged threaten-ingly around the doors of the building, awed for a time by the presence of the police, but at a little after one o'clock the attack began in earnest. An attempt was made to set the building on fire, but it was frustrated. Stones fell in showers upon the doors and windows. Many of the rioters had fire-arms and kept up a constant but ineffective fusillade, to which the police did not at first respond.

An attempt to storm the main entrance, the door being partly shattered, at last compelled the garrison to use their revolvers; and here fell the first of the rioters who were actually killed. Precisely how many were hit could not be known, but the ruffian who led the rush lay dead on the door-step, and others were borne away by their friends. Sergeant Burdick managed to send to Captain Cameron for help, but received for reply that there was none to send; and meantime the aspect of affairs grew darker and darker. At last, at about four o'clock, it became plain that the building could be held no longer. To remain was but to be massacred; and yet for a mere handful of thirty-five men, all told, to venture into the street was but to rush upon certain death. A much larger force was even then vainly struggling with the rioters, farther down the avenue, and twice as many had been driven from the enrolment office that morning. In this extremity a sort of " man-hole " was discovered in the rear wall of the factory, about eighteen feet from the ground, with a gutter-pipe below which would aid descent. It was barely large enough to let a man through, and all the Broadway Squad were six-footers; but they managed to perform the feat one after another, swinging themselves down undiscovered, and, making their way through back yards and over fences into Twenty-second Street, reached the Eighteenth Precinct station-house in that street on a keen run. Every man escaped ; but hardly was the last one out of the Armory before the doors were burst open and the mob poured in to plunder it, mad with rage to discover that their intended victims were beyond their reach.

There was some plunder to be had in the lower stories, but the drill-room on the upper floor was speedily thronged with half-drunken wretches, breaking open arm-chests, boxes, and closets, thoughtless of everything on earth but their seeming victory. So many were in the building as temporarily to weaken the fighting force of their comrades on the avenue, with whom the other police were vigorously contending. Some time passed, and many carbines were carried away, but the jam of rioters in the drill-room did not diminish.

Continually arriving squads of "off duty" men had reinforced the Metropolitans who were contending with the mob in that region, and a strong compact body of police was now seen fighting its way up Second Avenue. The rioters in the lower stories of the building received warning to come out. In an instant more they seemed to be trying in how many different places at once they could set the Armory on fire. The police made a vigorous charge which gave them possession of the front entrance, the principal means of escape for those who were yet inside. A double line of Metropolitans was quickly formed as a sort of human lane leading to the doorway, and as the plunderers rushed out, their arms full of carbines and other prizes, they were pitilessly clubbed down. It was a terrible gauntlet to run, and the police were in no condition to take prisoners. No man who came out of that doorway took any further share in the great riot. Living or dead, he was out of the fight for good, and was left on the pavement for such care as his friends might afterwards be able to give him. The responsibility of the matter was all his own. The intoxicated plunderers yet inside of the building were unaware of the fate of their friends, and no word of warning had reached the drill-room on the upper floor. Unknown to the police, it may have been still as full as ever of men when the wildly excited incendiaries performed their crazy task below.

It was a quarter before four o'clock when a telegram reached the Central Office:

" The mob have attacked the Armory corner of Second Avenue and Twenty-first Street. Two men shot dead. There is danger of firing the building."

It was precisely five o'clock when another message came, from the Eighteenth Precinct station :

" They have fired the Armory."

But only a very few, either then or afterwards, knew what was included in the meaning of the curt, business-like telegrams.

There was much combustible material on the lower floors of the doomed building. Workbenches and woodwork were saturated with oil, and the entire interior was of pine, seasoned and dry, and ready to burn like tinder. Parti-

tions, flooring, and stairways were quickly but one
sheet of roaring fire, and the stairways themselves
were but fiercely burning flues up which the
flames were rushing. The upper floor was cut
off in a few moments. It is even believed by
some that the rioters in the drill-room had for
some reason closed its doors upon themselves and
knew not what was coming. They certainly did
not know until it was too late, and the space
below them was little better than a furnace of
blazing pine. They were not called upon to
undergo any prolonged sufferings, however, even
of fear, for, as the beams sustaining it swiftly
yielded, the floor of the drill- room broke through
with a sudden crash, and all who were upon it
went down together into the pit prepared for
them by their crazy comrades. Not a man of
them escaped to tell the story ; and of the few
outsiders who knew anything about the matter,
none cared to speak of it for many a day. The
fierce excitement of the remainder of that week
prevented inquiry by any authority, and the
Police justly refused to take upon themselves any
blame for the sudden horror they were risking
their lives to prevent. It was one of the doings
of the Mob, and of the Mob only, and its awful

responsibilities rest solely upon them. ˙ All that was afterwards known of the horrible business was that, for some reason, the police took especial charge of the clearing away of those ruins before a new building was erected to replace the old one. There could be no trustworthy estimate made as to the number of victims, and not any is now known to have been made ; but charred human bones, devoid of flesh or form of body, were carried to the removal-carts in baskets and barrels, filled again and again, and one half-roasted body was found by the workmen who rebuilded the factory.

IV.

Down with Property!

BEFORE mid-day the disorders reported indicated that the combustible part of the population of New York was thoroughly ignited. There were mob-gatherings suddenly made at several widely separated localities simultaneously. It was not easy to decide which of them contained the greater promise of trouble to come.

The business community had been startled by a shock which had all the demoralizing effect of a sudden attack upon a sleeping camp. There was, nevertheless, a vast amount of steady courage displayed. The outnumbered and overworked police, in particular, did not waver for a moment. President Acton had at once made the needful requisition upon the military authorities for such aid as they might be able to give him. At an early hour of the day, General Wool had a personal interview with General Sandford, and afterwards another with Mayor Opdyke, and performed

with promptness the duty which devolved upon
him. He at once sent a dispatch-boat around to
all the thin United States garrisons of the fortifications around the harbor, directing the officers
in command of them to send to the city all the
men they could spare. These were at first
ordered to report for duty to General Sandford,
but the order was changed afterwards, and all the
United States troops on duty during the riot,
from the beginning, were immediately directed by
General Harvey Brown, as requested from hour
to hour by President Acton.

Similar messages went to the navy yard in
Brooklyn and to the United States armed vessels
lying in the harbor, of which there were several.
The responses were immediate, and detail after
detail swelled the " naval brigade," on the second
day of the riot, to a total of about seven hundred
men. These were for the greater part employed
in guard-duty at points of especial importance ;
but almost the first lesson received by the mob as
to the effect of musketry at short range was given
them by a company of U. S. marines on their
way to report as ordered. The rioters interfered
with the march, and the marines fired with ball-
cartridges at once, with wholesome effect.

Telegraphic reports of the aspect of affairs in New York City went freely to the War Office at Washington, and to the Executive Mansion itself. Necessarily, however, these first despatches conveyed an altogether fragmentary and inadequate idea of the impending peril, for neither the civil nor the military authorities of the city, nor its individual citizens, were yet prepared to comprehend the situation. It was not as yet imagined that the forces already at hand would prove unable to obtain a speedy mastery of the outbreak.

At Washington, also, there was a state of affairs which requires brief examination, that no hasty opinion should unjustly impute neglect or stupidity to the national government at such a crisis.

Every armed force at the disposal of the Commander-in-Chief, the President of the United States, had for several weeks been pushed to its uttermost exertion, in sieges, marches, battles; and with magnificent results. Among these results had been the victory at Gettysburg and the surrenders of Vicksburg and Port Hudson. Among the means necessarily called out and employed had been the State militia, or " National Guard," of New York, removing from that State for the time being all the organized and uniformed troops at the ordinary disposal of its Governor or its local authorities. These militia regiments were subject to the summons of the President, under the Constitution, but did not cease to be strictly "State troops," except as to obedience of general orders while on duty. Once out of the State, however, their return within any term or time for which they had been sent out was at the discretion of the President of the United States.

The records show that President Lincoln and Secretary Stanton, with their immediate co-laborers, were devoting every hour of time and every ounce of strength to the vast duties laid upon them. They were reorganizing shattered forces, filling up ranks depleted by the recent casualties and exhaustions, and they were urging on all men everywhere to the reaping of the mighty harvest brought within their reach at such a cost of blood. They were also eagerly looking forward to the results of the Draft, or conscription, in all the loyal States, for the men without whom Grant could not rapidly follow and crush the remaining Confederate armies in the West, nor Meade press with vigor upon the stubborn front yet presented by the beaten but unconquered Lee and the "Army of Northern Virginia."

The Richmond government was well known to be pushing its own conscription mercilessly, for corresponding reasons. In the words of President Lincoln's reply to Governor Seymour's request for a postponement of the Draft:

" We are contending with an enemy who, as I understand, drives every able-bodied man he can reach into his ranks, very much as a butcher drives bullocks into a slaughter-pen. No time is wasted, no argument is used. This produces an army which will soon turn upon our now victorious soldiers already in the field, if they shall not be sustained by recruits as they should be. It produces an army with a rapidity not to be matched on our side if we waste time to re-experiment with the volunteer system, already deemed by Congress, and, palpably, in fact, so far exhausted as to be inadequate ; and then more time to obtain a court decision as to whether a law is constitutional which requires a part of those not now in the service to go to the aid of those already in it ; and still more time to determine with absolute certainty that we get those who are to go in the precisely legal proportions to those who are not to go."

Governor Seymour should have been satisfied with that presentation of the case. It covered the whole ground of the nominal causes of the New York riot, and deprived the mob of all the excuses for their rising, then or afterwards made for them by their apologists.

The anxieties besetting the Administration were indeed great. Reports of probable resistance to the Draft did not come from New York City alone. Half-panic-stricken rumors thronged the telegraph-wires concerning initiatory or threatened disturbances in many other places. They came officially from other great and populous cities which serve as points of concentration for the pauper and criminal classes constituting the possible " mob element." It seemed likely that disorders were to be apprehended in communities less thoroughly organized for the preservation of the peace than New York was supposed to be, even in the absence of its militia regiments. The War Office was not without a fair excuse for the seeming tardiness of its action in the matter. It was handling a great many armies, in a great many fields, and the needs of this particular " engagement" with the public enemy were not well understood.

They were not at all understood in the city itself, for the very reason that the conscription was falsely set forth as the actual cause, when it was but the occasion, of the outbreak. The whole city knew that it contained no great number of men who were prepared to fight on that account.

Whatever may have been the organized nucleus of any part or segment of the general mob, no such body could have consisted, in any large proportion, of men who were actually drafted. No man, unless his name had come out of the wheel at the Third Avenue office on the previous Saturday, had any pretence of arming himself to avenge his own private wrong.

In preliminary preparations for the proposed mischief, class prejudices peculiarly un-American had been appealed to, and it is beyond question that these had great effect in stimulating the action of many. It is not easy for a European revolutionist transported to America to understand that human prosperity does not here, as in some other place known to him, stand for social oppression, or for caste privilege, or any kind of legalized robbery. Mere race prejudices, more despicable every way, were an incomparably more efficient and virulent stimulus of evil-doing. The mob made its most cowardly and felonious record in its treatment of unoffending colored people. Every vice of human nature seems to have been appealed to. Even the narrowness of perverted sectarian "religious" feeling was manifested by the bigoted ruffians who dishonored the Roman Catholic Church by sacking in its name the Five Points Mission, under Rev. C. W. Van Meter, as a Protestant intrusion upon ground sacred to the votaries of another creed. That was a purely local eruption, and all similar manifestations of ignorant and stupid sectarianism were rebuked in due time by the stern voice of Archbishop Hughes, as well as, throughout the riot, by the heavy clubs of Roman Catholic and Irish policemen.

The real nature of the outbreak began to manifest itself at the very earliest stage of the proceedings. It was a positive pleasure to coarse and brutal and cruel men and women to inflict pain upon the defenceless and unresisting. The beating, hanging, and torturing of negroes was to such beings a pleasurable excitement peculiarly fascinating. The momentary power to call upon all dram-sellers for unlimited potations of strong drink was a feature of the current temptation, the seductive power of which can hardly be exaggerated. Rum in all its forms, beginning as a danger, became in the end a most effective ally of the police and military. The free use of liquors did much to shatter and paralyze the energies of the rioters after its first work of arousing them to devilish frenzies began to die out in the third day's burning heats. The greed of plunder came to the front immediately, and recruited every thief in the city as a rioter; and the simply devilish lust of destruction came hand in hand with it.

Beyond all these, however, deeper and more powerful than all, but working in all and through all other causes and incentives of the riot, was the inbred hatred entertained by the European pariah and born criminal for all who are in any manner his visible superiors. The fact of that superiority is all that he can see, and he dreams not of emulation or imitation, which belong to the fundamental idea of genuine American citizenship. Since property and its ownership are a most visible and tangible manifestation of material superiority, the hatred includes both, or even transfers itself from the human possessor to the thing possessed, and the hater takes a strange pleasure in every work of property-mutilation or destruction. All well-dressed men and women were in peril if met by the mob of July, and all elegant houses were objects of its bitterness.

The intelligent American working-man more or less clearly understands that all existing property is in some sense or other his own and performs important uses for him. He knows that, whether it be nominally and legally in his individual possession or not, property in such a country as this cannot exist without him, nor can it be created without paying him tribute and doing something to better his condition. He knows perfectly well that if the production and existence of property at any time or place diminishes or ceases, the disaster occurs to him, and to him most oppressively. He holds in his own hands, as a citizen, absolute control of all property, and of the making and unmaking of all laws relating to it and to its possessors. Whatever may be true of other lands, the rich men of America hold every dollar of their riches only by the agreement and consent of the working-men that it is best and for the general good that so they should hold, and because of the general knowledge that no such riches can be destroyed and the cost of such destruction not be levied, by natural law as well as statute law, upon labor itself.

Destitute of all such thoughts or knowledges or trainings, or of any other, and oblivious of law, save as a hateful expression of detested power, the mob turned its blind rage against property and the owners thereof. While the enrolment office on Third Avenue was yet burning, another "nucleus" was leading a fast-increasing throng into Lexington Avenue and over towards the abodes of the prosperous and the evidently rich. Two beautiful private residences on the corner of Forty-sixth Street and Lexington Avenue were assailed and sacked and set on fire in sheer envy and bitterness excited by their elegance, and as an expression and seal of the purposes of the rioters.

The miscalculation by the promoters and leaders of the mob of the forces with which they were to contend did not appear to them at the outset. They seemed to themselves to be having matters very much their own way. Before noon of Monday they had beaten and driven the police in not less than a score of sharp contests, and they had captured and destroyed a United States enrolment office. They were jubilant, triumphant; and swarms of their previously hesitating sympathizers came out of their dens and coverts to join in the saturnalia of unpunished and seemingly unpunishable crime.

V.

Sacking an Orphan Asylum.

WHEN a man is taken hold of by some epidemic it does not appear that his whole body is instantaneously affected, neither do all his vital forces seem to rally at once to combat the disease. The time required may be short, however. And so it was with the great city and the sudden outbreak of the evil it contained.

The Metropolitan Police were hurrying from routine duties to their station-houses, and the " off duty" men were steadily coming in to be disposed of by the rapid generalship of President Acton.

Their details were numerically stronger now than at the beginning, and were swiftly marching hither and thither and fighting with splendid efficiency under the hot midsummer sun. Probably not more than eight hundred men were actually on duty in New York City itself at nine o'clock

that morning, scattered over their immense field
of operations, and it was late in the day before a
large force of them could be withdrawn from the
yet undisturbed precincts and concentrated upon
one point.

The first co-operation of the military was
obtained at the outset. The daily papers of
Saturday, July 11th, had contained the following
notification :

"HEADQUARTERS TENTH REGIMENT, N. Y. S. N. G.
OLD ARSENAL, July 11, 1863.

" General Orders, No. 7 : The above regiment is hereby ordered to form line at eleven o'clock on Monday
morning, the 13th inst., at the Arsenal, corner of White
and Elm streets, to leave for the seat of war.

" All of the members who have received their uniforms
will report punctually at the hour above stated. The
regiment having been recruited very rapidly for the last
few days, the Colonel commanding deems it necessary to
postpone leaving until Monday, on which day we will
positively depart for the seat of war.

" By order of John Missing, Lieutenant-Colonel commanding.

"J. C. RODRIGUEZ, *Adjutant.*"

The fact that this regiment consisted largely of
undisciplined recruits fully accounts for the fact
that they were deemed best adapted to the merely

garrison duties at once assigned them.   Nevertheless, their presence, "in line" and ready for
service, constituted a very important fact on
Monday morning.   They were a *militia* regiment,
of the New York State National Guard, which
had not been in effective condition at the time of
the President's call for temporary troops.   They
are not to be confounded with the " Tenth Regiment, New York State *Volunteers,*" afterwards
also employed in suppressing the mob.   Men
enlisting in the U. S. Regular Army were not
counted as of the quota of the State they came
from, or as fulfilling the obligations of that State
under any " call for troops."   Such quotas, prior
to the conscription, had been made up of " volunteers," each regiment organizing before leaving
the State to become a part of the National forces.
Every successive regiment of volunteers so organized was numbered as of the State it belonged
to, according to the order of its mustering-in.
Drafted men were never separately organized,
but were distributed among the old volunteer
regiments of their own States.

Colonel Missing, with two companies, numbering about one hundred men and soon reinforced to
three hundred, remained at the Arsenal at White

and Elm streets, to guard its peculiarly precious contents. They had with them a battery of three six-pounders and a sufficient number of artillery-men, and that depot of arms and ammunition was at once made secure. The police stationed at the Thirty-fifth Street Armory were at once relieved by about twenty-five men of the Invalid Corps and as many more detailed by Colonel Missing. Two more companies of the Tenth were at once marched to the Arsenal in the Central Park, where they were shortly reinforced by a third company. The disposition made of the remainder of the regiment cannot be accurately traced. The importance of so prompt a rescue of the several arsenals cannot be overestimated. The partial success of the mob on Third Avenue had supplied them with quite a number of serviceable weapons, but these were rendered comparatively useless by lack of ammunition of the proper sizes. A pocketful of cartridges which would not fit was of no more avail than so many marbles, and a carbine of the newest pattern was nothing but an iron club so long as it contained no cartridge.

General Wool immediately issued and circulated the following, which appeared in the next day's newspapers:

"HEADQUARTERS DEPARTMENT OF THE EAST,
NEW YORK, July 13, 1863.

"Special Order: All the troops called out for the pro-
tection of the city are placed under command of Major-
General Sandford, whose orders they will implicitly obey.
"C. T. CHRISTENSEN, *Assistant Adjutant-General.*"

This related, of course, to N. Y. State militia,
and volunteer regiments like the 10th N. Y. above
mentioned, and not to details from the U. S.
garrisons of the fortifications, who continued
under the direction of Brigadier-General Harvey
Brown of the regular army.

The residence of Mayor Opdyke had been an
intended point of attack from the first. It was
situated on Fifth Avenue, at a considerable distance from the scene of the outbreak.

The Mayor himself had taken no precautions
whatever; but, as soon as the Third Avenue affair was heard from, his friend and neighbor, Colonel B. F. Manierre, rallied a party of well-armed
citizens and took possession of the premises as a
garrison. The first gang of rioters which arrived
was neither very large nor altogether determined,
and it yielded temporarily to the combined effect
of a persuasive address from the Colonel and another from Judge Barnard, and a view of the rifle-

muzzles peering from the parlor windows. A strong squad of police shortly arrived and increased the defended appearance of the Mayor's house, so that another gang of would-be incendiaries retreated in like manner. Nevertheless, an attack would doubtless have been made by the better-organized mob afterwards dispersed by Inspector Carpenter's force on Broadway, but that on their appearance, in due succession, they found the proposed undertaking too perilous. Drawn up in front of the house was a detachment of United States Regular troops from Governor's Island, under Captain Wilkins of the U. S. Regular Artillery, numbering eighty-eight men, and dead sure to use ball-cartridges at the word " Fire." The prompt presence of these troops was a plain intimation of the wrath to come, but it was not heeded by the mob. Already the cry of " Down with the rich men !" was more and more freely uttered in all the gatherings of the rioters, and the Draft Act was heard of less and less. At twenty minutes past three o'clock the Police Central Office received this telegram :

"The mob are sacking and burning houses in Lexington Avenue near Forty-seventh Street. '

They were plundering more than burning, as only the two mentioned were then destroyed; but there was no one to resist them.

A curious example of the kind-heartedness which softens bad news was given in some telegrams which went out from the Central Office, simultaneously, at ten minutes past three o'clock. All were in response to inquiries.

To the Ninth Precinct:

"Inform Mrs. W. D. Kennedy and family that the Superintendent is not seriously hurt, and is improving."

To the First Precinct:

"The Superintendent is not dead, but seriously hurt."

To the Twenty-second Precinct::

"No: not dead. Hurt badly."

Throughout the afternoon futile efforts were made to call out the "exempt" firemen, in view of the increasing number and extent of the conflagrations raging. The firemen actually on duty did well, in many cases; but, as a whole, the conduct of that force continued to pile up good reasons for its subsequent disbandment.

At 4.35 P.M. it was telegraphed to the Central Office from the Twenty-first Precinct:

"The mob avow their intention of burning this station. Our connection by telegraph with you may be interrupted at any moment."

Ten minutes later, from the Twentieth Precinct it was announced:

"A very large mob now going down Fifth Avenue to attack *Tribune* office."

Affairs began to wear a gloomier aspect, for already at five minutes past four the Eighteenth Precinct station-house had reported:

"It is impossible for us to protect the building."

The garrison there held out bravely, and their assailants were temporarily repulsed by a reinforcement of police, only to return in greater numbers afterwards; and at last the station-house was captured by the mob and burned to the ground.

Something like greater concert of action, of a rude and clumsy sort, began to appear in the simultaneous movements of the rioters. They were operating in many places at once, and in each with more definite purposes and increasing

strength, insane and useless as the several purposes might seem to be.

At five minutes before five o'clock the Twenty-
ninth Precinct informed the perplexed watchers
at the Central Office:

" The mob has set fire to the corner of Broadway and
Twenty-ninth Street."

The vigorous efforts of President Acton for the
effective marshalling of his forces had already begun to bear good fruit. No large number of men
could be assembled to act as one body earlier
than 3 o'clock P.M., because of the constant demands for help at so many important points.

When gathered at last, it was needful to spend
some time in organizing for action ; but about two
hundred men under Inspector Daniel Carpenter
were ready for service when word came of the
movement upon the residence of Mayor Opdyke
in Fifth Avenue. The presence of the Regulars
there was unknown at the Central Office. Orders
were at once given for a movement of the whole
available force, and the Inspector and his captains, in President Acton's room, receiving instructions, asked of him, a little vaguely, " What
shall we do with our prisoners?"

" Prisoners?" almost screamed the angry President. " Don't take any! Kill! kill! kill! Put down the mob. Don't bring a prisoner in till the mob is put down."

The mob itself had taken no prisoners, and was killing and burning and torturing pitilessly.

The removing and care of prisoners was physically impossible at that hour.

In the open street, when Inspector Carpenter took command of his two hundred, he addressed them in the spirit of the orders he had received. He said to them :

" We are to meet and put down a mob. We are to take no prisoners. We must strike quick and strike hard."

He set them a splendid example at the first opportunity. The rioters who had retreated from the threatening rifle-muzzles which guarded the Mayor's house, were now marching down Broadway, increasing in numbers as they came, with the avowed purpose of sacking the Wall Street banks. They also declared their intention of taking, on their way, the Lafarge House, in which a large number of colored servants were employed. They were armed with clubs, pitchforks, iron bars, axes, swords, and many had muskets and pistols.

Wall Street at that hour would have been almost at their mercy. They had swelled to about one thousand men by the time they reached Amity Street. Vehicles of all kinds turned into the side-streets as the rioters were seen coming, and peaceable pedestrians fled in all directions, while shop-keepers hurriedly closed their doors and window-shutters.

Every colored man captured by the rioters on their march was mercilessly beaten, with reference to his share in the Draft Act, as "the cause of the war."

Inspector Carpenter and his men marched through Bleecker Street into Broadway, and confronted the mob just in front of the Lafarge House. There was no time for parley or hesitation, and the Inspector shouted :

"By the right flank ! Company front ! Double quick ! Charge !"

Then were seen the admirable results of discipline and drill. Steadily and promptly the lines of police, as they came into Broadway, swept out to "company front," filling the roadway from curb to curb. In perfect order, but with swift and sturdy steps, their heavy locust service-clubs in hand, the Metropolitans went forward,

6

the Inspector well in advance of the front line. Before them was a surging, howling mass, boiling with rage and hate, overflowing with brute strength, but without the effectiveness belonging to order.

All who saw that charge describe it as having been splendidly well done.

The mob resisted vigorously for a few moments, but the blows of the locust clubs were falling on them like rain. The ground was strewn with disabled ruffians, two of whom were afterwards found to have been killed outright. Onward pressed the Inspector and his men, preserving well their lines, the rear rank finishing such clubwork as the front rank passed along to them, but taking no prisoner. It was a hard fight, but the mob was broken, defeated, scattered.

This was the first regular battle of the mob in force with the police in force, and the complete victory won by the latter was of peculiar value in many ways. It demonstrated their discipline and fighting qualities, strengthened their confidence in themselves, and gave their opponents an excellent lesson in street-warfare. The organized "nucleus" of the mob in this fight carried a banner inscribed "No Draft," as well as an American flag, and both of these ·were captured by the police. It was nearly five o'clock before the struggle was altogether finished, and it cannot therefore be regarded as merely a blind rush and then a " walk-over."

During precisely the same hour another detachment of the mob, and a large one, had performed a deed of positively phenomenal cowardice and vindictive malice.

. The Orphan Asylum for Colored Children was on Fifth Avenue, its ample grounds extending from Forty-third to Forty-fourth Street. The building itself consisted of a four-storied central brick structure with wings of three stories, and was capable of accommodating five hundred children. At the hour when the attack was made upon it there were in it about two hundred children, all under twelve years of age, with the matrons, nurses, and other employés of the establishment. Some had already been sent away, for notice of coming peril had been given and partly believed, incredible as it must have seemed to any civilized man.

At about 4 o'clock P.M. word reached the asylum that a mob of about three thousand men was near at hand for its destruction. The Superintendent, Mr. William E. Davis, fastened the doors in the Fifth Avenue front while the children and women were gathering for a retreat. The doors resisted only just long enough for the little ones to make good their escape through the rear entrances, and then the mob rushed in to find that they had captured an empty, undefended building, guilty of the awful crime of having sheltered colored orphans under twelve years of age.

The work of pillage was rapidly and thoroughly performed, the bedding and the surplus clothing of the children being carried off as lawful prize, as were also their toys and trinkets and keepsakes. That, perhaps, was a protest against "property." The sacking was nearly done when Chief Engineer John Decker of the Fire Department arrived, all alone. He had heard of what was going on, and that the building was to be burned, and it was therefore within his province. He forced his way into the building boldly, but was knocked down twice while trying to argue with the ruffians he found there, and was roughly hustled out into the avenue. Here he found ten of his own men, and with these he again forced his way into the asylum. The furniture had been splintered and piled up, and fires had been lighted in several places on the first and second floors. These the firemen managed to scatter and extinguish, and for some few minutes they kept the incendiaries at bay; but other fires were kindling on the upper floors and these were beyond the reach of Decker and his men, and were speedily burning beyond any control whatever. It was clearly impossible to save the building, and a fierce rush of the mob carried Decker and his men out into the street.

Other firemen of several companies were now on the ground, but they were too late to accomplish anything with the fire, even if they had been permitted, and they were not. The wrath of the mob now turned vindictively against brave John Decker, and he came near losing his life. He would surely have been murdered but for the devotion and muscular strength of his men, who rallied around him and swore roundly that he should be reached only over their dead bodies. That being the case, he was permitted to remain alive.

As to the noble charity itself, it is well to record that it suffered no permanent hurt, although its building was burned to the ground. Hardly was the great riot put down before contributions of funds began to pour in from indignant men and women in all parts of the country, and the result was a new and better building, with a much larger endowment, in another locality.

During the burning of the orphan asylum the mob did not neglect the other houses in the vicinity, nearly all of which were private residences of the better class.

These, in swift succession, were broken into and plundered, their terrified inmates offering no resistance. To have done so would have been of no avail, and would but have invited more destruction.

The especial rage of the marauders seemed to be excited by every visible evidence of a life and culture higher than their own, and all articles of luxury or art were as sins to be wiped out. All costly furniture was to be marred or demolished or cast into the street. Anything light and portable, as jewelry, could be carried away; but a fine picture, a family portrait, or a pier-glass was sure to be destroyed. Many of the men were armed with hatchets, the plunder of hardware stores, and these were plied viciously upon carved furniture and pianos. There was an utter recklessness of the consequences of what they were doing, and a little white girl who stooped to pick up something pretty on the sidewalk was instantly killed by a heavy carved chair cast out of an upper window. The man who slew the child perhaps never knew what he had done, but her innocent blood was upon his grimy soul in spite of that.

The telegraph-wires leading to the Police Central Office had now been cut at many points. The process continued, in spite of much mending here and there by the daring telegraph corps of the Police Department, until only two main wires remained, and the existence of these was unknown to the rioters. From these two wires connections were made, outside and beyond, as fast as it could be done, and communications were maintained, often broken and incomplete, with the detached parts of the force and with the civil and military authorities of the city and the national government. Direct communication with the Mayor's office and the War Department was never broken. The Central Office was in a "state of siege," in some respects, during the afternoon and evening of Monday. When President Acton at last undertook to collect a stronger force at headquarters for decisive action, and to obtain more full reports of what was going on than could be sent to him by telegraph, he was confronted by a species of blockade. His responses were well imaged in one which was received from the Eighteenth Precinct at ten minutes past 6 o'clock P.M. :

"One of our officers just in says that not one of us can get to the Central Office, in uniform, alive. They will try in citizen's dress."

No better idea could be given of the completeness with which the streets of New York had that day passed under the control of the worst and vilest part of its heterogeneous population.

During the eventful hour between 4 and 5 o'clock P.M. of Monday yet another mob defeated a small force of military and police at the enrolment office on Broadway at the corner of Twenty-ninth Street. The books and papers had been removed earlier in the day, and the building was no longer related to the conscription. It was all the same. The government had occupied an office in it, and that was reason enough why all the property in that vicinity should be destroyed. The mob obtained entire control of the street, and prevented the approach of the fire companies. The building was a large one, and was to be burned to the ground; but its lower story was occupied as stores by tradesmen, and these were thoroughly plundered before fire was applied. One of the stores was a jeweller's establishment, and its contents were looted with more than common eagerness, in the name of the Draft Act. Here was a kind of property which for the greater part could be pocketed; but any of it too bulky or showy to be readily carried away was shattered to atoms or thrown into the flames with a barbarian zest worthy of the Huns of Attila.

At about the same hour of the day, the block of nearly new residences on Third Avenue at Forty-fourth Street for some reason attracted the attention of the rioters lingering in that neighborhood. These were thoroughly plundered first, and then were burned to the ground. There must have been, at times, a curious struggle in the minds of these wretches as to what particular mischief they had better turn their hands to next, after the completion of each successive enormity. The very magnitude of the city and the vastness of the property to be destroyed must have been a species of mental burden to them. What could they have done with their plunder in case they had succeeded in overpowering the police? These were indeed baffled and repulsed, but were by no means overcome. In spite of obstacles a good degree of concert of action among them was maintained, and their steady struggle with the mob did not cease for a moment. It was a continuous battle from street to street, and the plunderers were held in check. Had it been otherwise, the damage to the city which would surely have resulted cannot well be estimated, and would have been inflicted, like all that was actually done, without any imaginable profit to the vicious agents of destruction. These must in the end have been subdued by strong drink and starvation, among the wrecks they had made, unless more quickly destroyed by the bayonets whose coming they were inviting.

The whole "rising," judged by its course and conduct, was a kind of outbreaking insanity, little more; and it temporarily affected many who afterwards were quite willing to say nothing about it and remain sane and unclubbed for the remainder of their lives. There were preparations at this hour making, moreover, which were to add to the strong repentance occasioned by the club. Many men were to be given vivid memories of the strange appearance of a sheet of flame as it springs from a line of levelled rifles or a " moun tain howitzer," and others were to witness the awful effect of grape and canister from field-pieces.

The rising in the lower wards did not begin at an early hour. It was three o'clock in the after-noon of Monday before a mob assailed premises in Baxter Street occupied by colored people, and the attacking party was promptly dispersed by a detachment of police belonging to that—the Sixth —Precinct.

An hour or so later a similar attack was made on Crook's restaurant, in Nassau Street, because of the colored waiters employed there, and was defeated by the same force of Metropolitans. So was another attack made at half-past five o'clock on the dwellings of colored people in Pell Street, and another at six o'clock upon a build-ing at the corner of Leonard and Baxter streets occupied by about twenty colored families. Too many of the more determined leaders of the down-town " roughs" were with the mob in quarters where the promise of plunder was more enticing, and these anti-negro demonstrations lacked both in courage and leadership. Besides, a negro tenement-house could not be considered so closely connected with the Draft Act as could a jewelry establishment or a handsome residence.

Mayor Opdyke had a hard day's work that Monday, and the persistent attempts to sack his dwelling were a significant warning to him of what fate he might expect in case of his falling into the hands of the rioters. Not that he had in any manner injured them, individually or collectively. He was neither a policeman, nor a Draft official, nor a soldier, nor a negro, but he was the known representative of law, order, society, chosen by the people so to be ; and he must die for that fact, and for that fact only, if the mob could get at him. He remained all day at his post of duty at the City Hall, although at times it became one of no little apparent danger. In the evening he established his headquarters at the St. Nicholas Hotel. To him was due much of the immediate efficiency of the forces, military and other, which were now fast gathering. None of these were yet in shape to be sent to the aid of the Metropolitans. The latter were as yet without reinforcements so far as actual street-fighting went, but were nevertheless vastly relieved and strengthened by what was being done behind their lines. From the very beginning, energetic attention was given to the protection of shipping at the wharves; of hotels; of important trade localities like the " dry-goods district," west of Broadway; of banks and moneyed institutions; of the financial district designated by " Wall Street." To illustrate : the company of men to which the writer of this book was attached was that day stationed successively in front of the Sub-Treasury; at the Custom-house; at a point near the Astor House ; and, after indefinite marching, was posted for the greater part of the night in the corridors of the Metropolitan Hotel. In each post save the last it was relieved by a larger, better armed, and more effective body of men. Capable military men were ready at once to take charge of hasty levies, and of these the greater number had previously seen service in the army.

The military force gathered at the Seventh Avenue Armory by Monday evening was reported as follows by Colonel Henry Moore, Forty-seventh N. Y. Volunteers, commanding :

" Several twelve-pounder mountain howitzers from Governor's Island, with artillerists; detachment of Tenth N. Y. State militia under Major Seeley; detachment of Twelfth Regular U. S. Infantry, from Fort Hamilton

Captain Franklin; ditto, Third Regular U. S. Infantry, from Governor's Island, Captain Wilkins; ditto, Invalid Corps, from Riker's Island; ditto, — N. Y. State Volunteers, Captain Lockwood."

Total, about one thousand men, armed and equipped. Colonel Moore was relieved at his own request, and was succeeded by Colonel Robert Nugent, Deputy Provost-Marshal-General.

Two companies of U. S. Regular Infantry, under Lieutenants Wood and Penny, reached the police Central Office at 11 o'clock P.M. General Harvey Brown spent the evening at the Central Office, and at a late hour had a conference with General Sandford.

Governor Horatio Seymour was not in the city on Monday, and was as yet ignorant of the exact state of affairs, as appears by the following letter, afterwards printed :

" NEW YORK, 13th July, 1863.

"MY DEAR SIR : I have received your note about the Draft. On Saturday last I sent my Adjutant-General to Washington for the purpose of urging a suspension of the Draft, for I know that the city of New York can furnish its full quota by volunteering. I have received a despatch from General Sprague that the Draft is suspended. There is no doubt that the conscription is postponed. I learn this from a number of sources. If I get any information of a change of policy at Washington. I will let you know.   Truly yours,

(Signed)   " HORATIO SEYMOUR.

" *Hon. Samuel Sloan, President of the Hudson River Rail-road, New York.*"

There appears to be no doubt that some official of the War Department was talking unad_visedly upon this subject and misleading the Governor and others. Two days later the chief conscription official of the District of New York received advices which led him to print the following, only to have it instantly disavowed by his superiors :

" The Draft has been suspended in New York City and Brooklyn.

(Signed)   " ROBERT NUGENT,
    " *Colonel and Assistant Provost-Marshal-General.*"

The mob had choked it off for that week, but the Administration had not for one moment proposed its suspension by any other process, as President Lincoln's reply to Governor Seymour testifies,

VI.

A Memorable Night.

THE days of July are long, and it was now near sunset of the first day of the riot. The militia and the disbanded volunteers were gathering rapidly and spontaneously at their accustomed places of rendezvous. Sufficient numbers of them had already assembled to provide tolerable garrisons for the several arsenals, armories, and public buildings. Some of the larger hotels, warned by the attempt upon the Lafarge House, had taken measures for self-protection. The gashouses were properly cared for. Something had been done for the ship-yards and shipping, and for exposed places along the water-front. A gunboat lay at the foot of Wall Street, with her guns trained to sweep it, while another lay off the Battery Park, in like manner, and several in front of the Navy Yard. The Sub-Treasury building, the Custom-house, the Stock Exchange, were well protected. Numbers of stalwart citizens were continually offering themselves to the police authorities as volunteer "special" policemen for this occasion, and all suitable persons were at once sworn in and armed.

The prospect for further reinforcements on Tuesday was excellent, but the immediate present was dark enough.

The plain indications of a hot evening's work and a night of tumult and probable disaster came pouring into the Central Office from almost every corner of the city. Among so many demands, all apparently imperative, it was necessary for President Acton to make prompt selections of such as were of greatest importance to the general safety. He was also compelled to restrict his operations to the capacity of his as yet limited force. A large number of his men had been fighting and marching in the hot sun all day, and he knew that there was somewhere a limit to physical endurance.

The men in the Eighteenth Precinct were maintaining their good fight, but they were hard pressed and were calling loudly for help. At ten o'clock they were telegraphed :

"Hold on. Carpenter will soon be there."

And again in a few moments:

" Is everything all right?"

They returned for answer:

" A great crowd at corner of Twenty-second Street and Second Avenue."

The police had not for some hours been able to get anywhere near the scene of their morning's discomfiture and the as yet almost unknown holocaust of self-burned marauders. Few of the crowd then gazing upon the smoking ruins of the Armory building had any idea that the bones of men were charring among the coals and ashes before them.

All that part of the riot regarded itself as having gained a complete and final victory over the police, although at a heavy cost of killed and wounded. The latter fact did not interfere at all with the prevailing sense of triumph, but it inevitably added to the growing bitterness of feeling. It added to the ranks of the " mob " proper many recruits from that part of our imported population whose European experience has taught it to regard all order-keeping authority and power as its natural enemy. This is the strictly revolutionary, anarchist, communist element, whose dense ignorance or perversity unfit it for free institutions like our own. It is a fruit of long ages of undue repression and misgovernment in other lands, and America helplessly receives it.

In no other part of the city was there a gathering so large, numerically, at that hour, as that on Second Avenue; but every drinking-place in the lower part of the city served as a rendezvous of sedition. Peaceable men were for the moment overawed, and the ruffians who talked violence had the conversation to themselves. Disorder broke loose in spots, as of a social disease coming to the surface. It was out of the question for the Metropolitans to attend to any part of their ordinary business of keeping the peace, for a solitary policeman, anywhere, would but have been a victim instantaneously sacrificed.

At six o'clock a telegram came to the Central Office from the Eighth Precinct:

" Can't you send five or ten men here ? They are driving all the niggers out of the ward, as soon as they show on the street."

Help had already been sent and had nearly ar-

rived, for in fifteen minutes more the sa
cinct telegraphed :

" All quiet. ' Crowd dispersed."

This referred to some one of the many
and it gave no estimate of the clubbing
dispersing it.   Neither could any one mc
guess at the amount of suffering wantc
flicted by the brutes who were "driving
niggers out of the ward."

At the same hour, six o'clock, came th
the Twenty-second Precinct :

" The children from the Colored Orphan As
here for protection, having been turned out of
the mob."

Two hundred poor little things, under
years of age, in a nominally civilized com
requiring armed protection, after their ho
been burned down !

At ten minutes before seven o'clock Pɪ
Acton inquired of the much-beleaguered
eenth Precinct :

" How are matters in your precinct ?"

and obtained for answer :

" The mob is in all the streets—most everywhɛ

This meant neither more nor less than that the police had been overwhelmingly outnumbered. They had been driven out of the streets, and the rioters in all that region were having things their own way.

The resources of the department were already strained to their uttermost, and but small reinforcements could be sent. Full two hours later, after the long and hard struggle had swayed back and forth with varying features of successes and reverses; the inquiry was again repeated:

"For Captain Cameron: How are matters in your precinct?"

The reply came almost instantly, " Very bad ;" and was quickly followed by the ominous question:

" Shall we shut up shop ?"

That was a hard and bitter pill for President Acton, but there was no help for it. He had no men to send, and the only possible reply was a curt and surrendering " Yes." The station-house " shop" was shut up, and the victorious rioters in due season burned it down ; but the Metropolitans kept right on with their fight for the possession and control of the precinct.

At ten minutes before seven o'clock the condition of affairs in the Fourth Precinct for the first time became precarious, and a telegram came from it:

"Great excitement in this ward. Only a section of men here. Ask inspector if they can't remain. Much needed. Station-house being stoned. Muskets in use."

Help was sent. Forty minutes later, in response to the stereotyped question, "How are things in your ward?" it was responded: "Riotous condition;" to be followed in fifteen minutes by:

"The rioters are attacking colored boarding-houses, robbing them and setting them on fire. I have not force enough to prevent it."

Communication with the Central Office was severed, and the next message, at 8.25 o'clock, came by way of the Twenty-sixth Precinct:

"The Fourth wants help bad."

By nine o'clock the Fourth could again use the wires, and was compelled to report:

"Things awful bad here. Inspector D. C. [Carpenter] here with big force, but excitement increases. Two colored men brought in almost dead."

There had been many such victims whom the police had not been able to rescue and bring in. They were hunted down like so many wild animals, and the cowardly ferocity of the mob was growing by what it fed on, in preparation for the horrors which were to follow. The requirements of the struggle in this region were such as to compel a concentration of force which weakened the police at other points and places.

The troubles in the First Precinct began in the afternoon, moderately, but did not assume a dangerous aspect until after supper-time. At seven o'clock a telegram came from it to the Central Office:

"Tell Captain Marlow there is a riot in this ward."

It was an hour when nothing could be done for that locality. Even the force already there was needed elsewhere. Only fifteen minutes later they were answered:

"Leave a few men and take the rest to the *Tribune* office."

There had been full warning given, throughout the day, of the intention of the mob to sack and burn the *Tribune* etablishment. It was a high

compliment to that journal that it should so be
singled out for destruction by the powers of
darkness. It was an expression by the mob of a
semi-intelligent political animosity which almost
disappeared with this effort and with the subsequent burning of Colonel Nugent's house and
Postmaster Wakeman's, and the breaking of
Mayor Opdyke's windows.

The *Times* newspaper was at this time as ob-
noxious as the *Tribune* in its politics and its course
towards the mob, but none of the rioters had ever
read either, and it was easier to concentrate malice
upon one pile of bricks. And then the *Tribune*
was a newspaper which for many years had been
the special advocate and defender of the negroes.
It was Horace Greeley; and all genuine anti-Draft
men had good cause to hate so strong a " war-
for-the-Union" man and abolitionist as he. As
for other mob elements, he very well imper-
sonated all that they opposed, and they had
already done their best to catch and kill him.
His escape from their hands had been a narrow
one.

There were many reasons why the *Tribune* as a
journal was a standing offence to the criminal
classes. The building and presses of such an

institution were fit only to be burned, and its editors and other workmen were proper subjects of mob-violence.

The locality of the *Tribune* building, opposite the City Hall, was in many respects exposed. The open area in front of it was wide and could be rushed into by bodies of men through either or all of several thoroughfares.

There had been many small gatherings of roughs in that vicinity during the afternoon, but they had been awed by the police at and about the City Hall. The course of events could be but little more than closely watched, but this precaution had been carefully taken. A considerable body of Metropolitans was gathered and was well in hand, in view of what was known to be coming. They came very near to being too late, carefully as their movements had been planned. At five minutes before eight o'clock it was announced from the Twenty-sixth Precinct:

" The *Tribune* building attacked and no force here."

There was half an error in that, so nearly had the force arrived.

The mob obtained but a brief and partial victory. They swarmed into the lower story of the establishment, doing what damage they could, and they had already kindled a fire on the floor as a token of their purposes, when the Metropolitans were upon them. Only ten minutes after the first warning despatch, it was supplemented by :

" All right.   Our men this moment arrived.   Drove the mob, and after them across the street."

That was well enough to begin with, and the building was saved ; but the counter-rush of the mob drove the police in turn.   Still, at 8.15 came once more the sad but hopeful assurance :

" *Tribune* office gutted, but our men hold the mob at bay, and will hold them.   Our men are all in possession of every street now."

Wherever the police in force could meet their opponents, they were sure to give a good account of them ; but small squads and single officers were only so much wasted material.   The numerical superiority of the rioters was too great, and they did not hesitate one instant in the use of weapons.   They could be counted now by the thousand, and they were pressing into their ranks the hitherto doubtful and unwilling.   Every man

falling into their hands and refusing to become
one of them was a proper person to be robbed or
knocked down and pounded to a jelly.

At 8.25 the Sixth Precinct reported :

"There is a large crowd tearing down colored dwellings
in Park Street. Send some help."

Ten minutes later it was telegraphed from the
Thirteenth Precinct :

"The mob has fired Duffy's place, No. 429 Grand
Street."

This was the enrolment office of that district.

The trouble in the First Precinct began to lull a
little, its rioters drifting towards the upper wards ;
and at 8.50 P.M. an inquiry: ·

"How are things with you ?"

was answered :

"Quiet at present. We are taking in a good many
colored lodgers for protection."

Such was the case at every station-house in the
city, and the poor hunted creatures sought a
hiding-place within any house whose white occu-
pant had the courage and humanity to give them

shelter. There was no small risk taken by the Good Samaritans whose doors were opened to the trembling fugitives from blind brutality and cowardly persecution.

The Tenth Precinct was commonly understood to be as yet almost exempt from noteworthy disturbances, and as late as 9.55 the Thirteenth Precinct operator cheerfully declared :

" There is no trouble in the Tenth Precinct yet."

Alas for the accuracy of his information ! More than half an hour earlier, the Tenth Precinct had telegraphed the Central Office, " Send some men forthwith ;" and when asked, " What is up ?" responded :

" A crowd is here and are going to destroy this station."

Help reached them in time to prevent such a conclusion, and the mob at that point was kept at bay for the remainder of the night.

The militia officers and the officers of the several disbanded volunteer organizations of New York and Brooklyn had not been idle during the day. In the latter city there had been no disorder of sufficient extent to interfere with the Draft, and it had proceeded without interruption. It continued to do so until it was completed, and 14,208 men had been duly selected out of an enrolment of over 30,000.

The different commanders did more than consult among themselves. The following notification, for instance, among others was rapidly circulated during the afternoon and evening of Monday, and was printed in the papers of the next morning:

"NATIONAL ZOUAVES: Attention! The officers and members of the Tenth Regiment, New York Volunteers, who are willing to assist in the enforcement of the laws are requested to meet at 525 Broadway, Armory of Thirty-seventh New York State Guards, as early this day as possible, in full uniform.

"JOHN E. BENDIX, *Colonel.*"

The following was also issued and printed in like manner:

"HEADQUARTERS EIGHTH REGIMENT, N. Y. S. N. G.

"The members, ex-officers, and ex-members of this regiment, in the city, including troops, are requested to meet at the Armory to-morrow, July 14th, at 8 o'clock A.M. By order of Maj. LEANDER BUCK,

"D. B. KEELER, Jr., *Adjutant.*"

The New York City Board of Aldermen, in response to the summons of the Mayor, had attempted to get together at noon, and did so at half-past 1 o'clock P.M., but were unable to obtain a quorum for the transaction of business.

General Sandford and his immediate military advisers had not been idle, and in response to a summons issued by him at an early hour, and industriously circulated throughout the day, a meeting of officers and ex-officers of all sorts took place at the Seventh Regiment Armory, over Tompkins Market, on Monday evening at eight o'clock.

It was attended by about two hundred gentlemen, every one of whom came to it at the imminent peril of his life.

Active measures were adopted for the enrolment and organization of volunteers in various parts of the city, and suitable commanders were designated. The commanding general was thereby relieved of a mass of work and responsibility, a rapid gathering of forces was secured, and President Acton and his Metropolitans were assured of inestimable reinforcements.

It must not be overlooked, however, that several of these officers were actively engaged already in reorganizing their former commands or forming new ones, with a view to re-enlistment in the army. They had therefore considerable bodies of men, veteran soldiers for the greater part, enrolled and ready to assemble for active service. A similar state of preparation, followed by corresponding promptness of action, could not exist in any time of peace. It does not exist now, and will not henceforth. There are many capable officers in the city of New York and in other cities, but they have no such reserves of effective soldiery, well acquainted with them, trusting them as leaders, and ready to rally at their summons. As was soon to appear, many of the better known commanders had only to send word to the rank and file at their homes as if at "quarters," and the men "turned out and fell in."

The evening grew darker, save in the neighborhoods of the burning buildings. It was intensely and oppressively warm, yet cloudy, the heavy air redoubling the fatigue of all exertion. Some relief came at about eleven o'clock, in the shape of a drenching storm of rain, which did good work in putting out fires and scattering crowds of men, as well as in cooling the atmosphere.

At about half past nine o'clock the Fifteenth Precinct sent word to the Central Office:

"A large crowd coming down Broadway."

And other alarming messages were constantly arriving from other directions. It was to the last degree harassing and perplexing: so large a field to fight over with so small a force and so numerous and venomous an enemy. Sheer exhaustion was having some effect upon the strength of the mob. So was drunkenness. So did the rain have, when at last that came. Nevertheless, at no hour of that gloomy night did the struggle really cease for one moment. There was a striking illustration of this at a quarter before twelve, midnight. One of the earlier exploits of the mob on the western side of the city, low down-town, had been to capture an unoffending negro man and, after enjoying the pleasure of beating and kicking him, to hang him to a tree, with a fire kindled under his feet. They exhausted the full delight of torturing the poor fellow to death, and no force of police had as yet been able to approach the spot where yet a gloating throng drank in the ecstasy of seeing the hanging horror. To many of them it must have been almost as good as having helped to pound him for being black.

At 11.45 P.M. President Acton telegraphed the Twenty-eighth Precinct, in which partial quiet was believed to have been obtained: " Is the body of that negro hanging yet?" And the answer was, "Yes." "In what street?" asked Mr. Acton. "Clarkson, near Hudson."

"Take it down forthwith; and if you can't, let me know."

The presence of such a "trophy" was disgrace enough to the city to warrant a vigorous effort for its removal; but at 12.25 the requested report arrived, and it was not encouraging:

"The men have just returned. The mob won't let us have the body."

The malice which lasted so long, after a painful death had deprived the wretches of their poor victim, is a sufficient declaration of the fact that these fiends in human form are in no wise to be confounded with "American working-men." This conduct left no stain upon

8

us, for they were not and are not of us. Whether born on the soil or born elsewhere, they
were foreigners to every idea and hope and
instinct which at all belongs to this free country. In shooting them down, afterwards, the
police and military were destroying a hellish
raid from the slums of Europe. The bodies
of that and other murdered negroes were afterwards recovered and decently interred.

The rioters were still attempting, here and
there, to keep up a pretence of political feeling;
and in the course of the night, towards morning, they sacked and burned the residence of
Abram Wakeman, the city postmaster. He
had nothing to do with the Draft, truly, but
he was a well-known Republican politician, a
government official, a man of property, and
an open and avowed supporter of the "Lincoln despotism." It was an excuse, to be sure ;
but they had already plundered and destroyed
other fine residences without any excuse at all,
and need not have been particular in selecting
the postmaster's house, unless because it contained much that was worth stealing.

There was more or less of local outrage and
unrecorded "skirmishing" during all the re-

mainder of the night. There were many attacks upon the dwellings of colored people.

There were burglaries and highway robberies and beatings and other cruelties in many places. No minuteness of detail is possible, nor is it necessary.

The press reporters did as much of their accustomed duty as they might, at the peril of their lives if detected in so doing by the mob; but there were huge districts into which not one of them could or did penetrate, to ascertain the evil there going forward. The police did not so much as attempt to keep their usual record of occurrences. In fact, from the beginning to the end of the riots, not one solitary police captain found time to make up and send in his regulation "morning report," and the books of that department are almost a blank as to the deeds of those memorable days when every Metropolitan was too busy with his club to use a pen.

VII.

Tuesday's Hard Fight.

[T is not to be supposed that the leading spirits
    of the rioters, in their many detached bands,
ailed to hold consultations at the end of Mon-
lay's apparent victory. So far as they were able
o discern, the city lay almost at their mercy,
nd they well knew that only a part of their re-
ources had been drawn out into open activity.
`hey believed themselves to have already beaten
he police ; the militia were out of town, and
hey had no idea of any improvised military force.

The riot-fever was spreading fast among all
he classes morally prepared for its infection, and
arried with it the strong delusion that with
ne more vigorous push the mob would be in
omplete control of Manhattan Island, and able
ɔ dictate terms to all authorities, city, State, or
Iational. Precisely this view of the case was
penly propagated by their emissaries the follow-

ing morning among the working-men of several well-known concerns. Wonderful visions of almost unlimited plunder and self-indulgence were before them, and they were not without visible grounds for their mad fantasies. The man of criminal life and governed by animal instincts is necessarily a mentally short-sighted man. His ideas go but little beyond what he can touch at any time, and in fierce excitements like the one these banditti had stirred themselves into his calculations grasp only such things as he can see. He may nevertheless take in exaggerated conceptions of deeds reported to have been done around the next corner.

Apart from all mutual consultations, plans, and preparations, the activities of the rioters had been sleepless. Their gatherings began to assume threatening proportions before daybreak, and again their agents were on hand at the earliest hours of work. They passed from place to place rapidly, notifying all laborers and working-men to " quit" on peril of violence, and all establishments employing them to close on pain of destruction.

President Acton could have given them a mass of useful information that morning if they had called upon him. He could have told them truths which, if in their insanity they could have believed or heeded, might have saved several hundreds of human lives. He was straining every nerve to prepare all things for the heavy day's work before him. He was determined to make it a thorough one, and had estimated its magnitude fairly. Not for one minute of that turbulent, feverish night had he closed his eyes in sleep, or ceased his vigilant study of every part and parcel of his field of action. He could not, of course, obtain detailed reports of events, but he seems to have divined almost instinctively the condition of those areas from which he could obtain no positive information, and to have acted unhesitatingly upon his keen professional judgment of probable necessities. He knew somewhat of the forces which were gathering for his assistance, and took the coming of them all for granted. He was already making preparations to receive, to care for, and especially to feed, as many as might come. These preparations, the commissariat included, he had put into the efficient hands of Seth C. Hawley, chief clerk of the Police Department.

President Acton had already been compelled to meet and deal with some very remarkable people in the character of would-be advisers. Among them had inevitably come a full proportion of professional politicians, sturdy demagogues, and of cowardly compromisers who were yet not destitute of social standing. He had answered each and all as best he could, and had gone straight forward. It was a time for prompt energy, and President Acton was not the man to stop at trifles or technicalities. He did not wait for "proclamations," nor for any other authority than such as the mob itself was giving him. He roundly answered sundry legal objections to the action he was taking and proposed to take by asserting that he had no time just then to hunt up the law governing such cases. He must put down the mob, he said, law or no law, and attend to all the technicalities after order should be restored. This was very good law indeed, and was afterwards so held to be by the courts, but it was well that a man of excellent, cool, incisive judgment, as well as unhesitating decision, was intrusted with the enforcement of such a temporary dictatorship. If a building then or at a later hour was required as "quarters" or for any other public purpose, his men were ordered to take it and use it. If a stock of provisions was demanded for the feeding of his forces, of any sort, and the owner's fears or cupidity made him refuse to sell for such purposes, the police were merely instructed to "take a strict account of every ham," but to carry off the last pound of the eatables needed. There were some curious and even grotesque results of this management.

Among the other buildings rescued from destruction during Wednesday's warfare was the African Methodist Church on Thirty-fifth Street. It was saved only after a severe fight with the rioters, who were trying to tear it down or burn it. Its continued security absolutely required that it should be garrisoned, and its locality as well as size made it admirably suited for barrack purposes. Soldiers and "specials" were therefore quartered in the meeting-house, as many as it would hold; and such a number of men could not eat and sleep in such a place even for a few days without rendering it somewhat the worse for wear. No needless damage was done; but, as a matter of course, when all was over, the spiritual magnates of the church brought in a bill against the city for all the detriment the property had sustained from the mob. This was justice, and

it was law, and the bill was duly paid ; but it first
required a little "auditing." It contained noteworthy items. The church carpets had been
pretty well worn before the mob and the soldiery
came, but an allowance was asked for new carpets throughout. After some demur this was
passed, and the new carpets were provided.
There had been some kind of a Sunday-school
library, also in a battered condition, and the
worthy elders inserted a sum sufficient for the
purchase of a new one, on the ground that the
unrighteous police, soldiery, and "specials" had
read up forever all there was left of the old.
This too it was decided to allow, in the hope that
the force had obtained some benefit from their
reading. But the next demand was a stumbling-
block. It gravely assumed that the city was responsible for the peculiar species of "summer vacation" enforced upon the church by the mob,
and called upon the city treasury for the "estimated and probable amount" of three consecutive
Sunday collections from such congregations as
might, could, would, or should have assembled in
that building and put something into "the plate"
in case there had been no riot, and if they had
not been too badly scared to hear preaching

earlier than the first Sunday in August. There was a good deal of quiet fun upon one side of the argument and some pious grumbling on the other, but the omitted "collections" were not reimbursed by the city treasury. That church and the Orphañ Asylum both made money by the mob, but in somewhat different ways.

The idea that the riot was an anti-Draft riot and nothing else was wonderfully strong. The illusion prevailed that if the "conscription" could in some manner be wiped out the riot would subside. The public patient was not doctored for the right disease. A curious example of judicial demagogism was presented for future avoidance, at an early hour of Tuesday, by City Judge John H. McCunn, whose name was afterwards to become better known to the country through his relations with the Tweed Ring.

A prepared case was brought before him, of a man conscripted on Saturday, July 11th, and the judge gravely decided it against the Government of the United States, reading a prepared "decision,"—immediately printed in the newspapers,—in which he averred the Draft Act to be unconstitutional and void and inoperative. The judge's decision did not deter its supposed beneficiaries from doing an immense amount of larceny that very day.

The newspapers of Tuesday morning were full to overflowing with accounts of the disturbances of the previous day, and with the muster-calls of military commanders. The men gathered on Monday had all been assigned to duty, and those who now followed them were organized and set to work as they came. It required some courage to come from any district in a large part of the city. The mob held almost undisputed possession of their yesterday's battle-fields, at the beginning of the day, and were disposed to interfere with opposition recruiting.

The Metropolitans could not but be encouraged by their prospects for reinforcement, and their own operations were already such as promised important results. At 7.45 A.M. the following message reached the Central Office by way of the Twentieth Precinct Station:

" *To Commissioner Acton :*

"I have the honor to inform you that General Sandford sent to the scene of riot two six-pounders, twenty-five artillerists, and one hundred and fifty infantry, under command of Colonel O'Brien. They were well armed, and left at precisely quarter before seven.

"A. HAMILTON, A. A. C."

The men referred to were made up of both volunteers and militia, and did good service; but Colonel O'Brien was to pay bitterly for his ready patriotism in leading them.

Other advices of military operations and purposes came faster and faster, from that hour onward; and so did reports of the movements of the swelling mob.

It was but ten minutes later when there arrived from the same precinct:

"As the Mayor calls for special policemen, a citizen here offers five hundred clubs for the emergency."

All the morning papers contained the following:

"PROCLAMATION BY THE MAYOR.

"MAYOR'S OFFICE, N. Y. CITY,
July 14, 1863.

"In view of the riot now existing in this city, I do hereby request all loyal citizens to report at the Headquarters of the Police, No. 300 Mulberry Street, this day, to be sworn in and enrolled as special policemen for the restoration of law and order. All who shall not thus enroll themselves are requested to continue their usual avocations.

(Signed)   "GEORGE OPDYKE, *Mayor*."

The following was also printed in connection with the Mayor's proclamation:

"The veterans who have returned from the field of battle have again an opportunity of serving not only their country, but the great emporium of New York against the threatened dangers of a ruthless mob.

"The Commanding General of the Eastern Department trusts that those who exhibited so much bravery in the field of battle will not hesitate to come forward at this time to tender their services to the Mayor, to stay the ravages of the city by men who have lost all sense of obligation to their country as well as to the city of New York.

(Signed) "JOHN E. WOOL, *Major-General.*"

The veterans, men of military training and habit of mind, came forward rapidly ; and the fact that greater numbers of unmilitary citizens did not instantaneously do so was not without its reasonable excuses. The public generally knew little of the extent of the riot, and had great confidence in the police. It was also blind to the condition of its military resources. Moreover, men who had homes and families ; all fathers and brothers, and those near of kin or close in friendship, were thinking most anxiously of the protection required by their own doorways. Business men of every grade turned their first attention to the security of their shops, offices, stores, warehouses, and factories, justly considering that these were in hourly peril.

However individually brave and public-spirited so great a mass of men may be, their very numbers are in the way of their accepting the personal duty of dropping all other responsibility and of turning out into the streets as fighting men. Besides, the streets were known to be infested with roving gangs and bands of rioters, and no man could predict at what place he would or would not meet with one of these. The thoroughfares leading to designated mustering-places were likely to be full of peril to all well-dressed men who might be suspected of being on their way to volunteer, or of being in favor of enforcing the Draft, or of having in their pockets something worth stealing. It was already well understood that a plundered man was sure to be at least half murdered before his plunderers were done with him.

Among the military notices published on Tuesday morning were the following:

" HEADQUARTERS FIRST DIVISION, N. Y. STATE MILITIA. NEW YORK, July 13, 1863.

"The ex-officers of this Division and of the United States Volunteers, now in this city, who are disposed to assist in preserving the peace of the city, are requested to meet at the Seventh Regiment drill-rooms, over Tompkins Market, this evening at eight o'clock.

(Signed) "CHARLES W. SANDFORD, *Major-General.*"

One meeting had been held, and this call for a second had its good results.

"HEADQUARTERS FIRST DIVISION, N. Y. STATE MILITIA.
NEW YORK, July 13, 1863.

"Special Order No. 37 : All officers, non-commissioned officers, and privates late of the Two Years' Volunteer Service, now in the city, are especially requested to assemble forthwith at Central Hall, No. 174 Grand Street, and report to Colonel William H. Allen for temporary volunteer duty.

" By order of Major-General Charles W. Sandford.

" ALEXANDER HAMILTON, A. A. C."

Colonel J. M. Davis, late of the " Harris Light Cavalry," also received at the Seventh Regiment Armory all who preferred to report to him for organization, both officers and privates. At the Division Armory the following gentlemen had established " headquarters," and were receiving and enrolling their former subordinates and others : Colonel Allen, First Regiment, N. Y. S. Vols.; Lieutenant-Colonel Ashley, Thirty-seventh N. Y.

S. N. G.; Colonel Taylor, Fourth N. Y. S. Vols.; Major Wales, Seventeenth Chasseurs; Colonel Howard, Twelfth Volunteer Heavy Artillery. Notices similar to those already quoted had been issued and circulated, and were afterwards published in the papers of the 15th, by Lieutenant-Colonel Robert F. Allason, old Thirty-eighth N. Y. S. N. G.; Colonel E. Jardine, Ninth N. Y. S. Vols., better known as the "Hawkins Zouaves;" Colonel Frank Jones, Thirty-first N. Y. S. Vols.; and officers from other similar organizations. There was a prompt response, especially from some, for example the Hawkins Zouaves, because the regiment called upon was already in a more or less advanced state of re-enlistment and reorganization with a view to renewed service at the front. Early on Tuesday morning began the organization of the "Minute Men," at the Seventh Regiment Armory, under direction of General Sandford. Into this body several of the regimental fragments first gathered were readily absorbed; and the process was so rapid that a full regiment could at once be mustered and assigned to duty under command of Colonel Cleveland Winslow of the Duryea Zouaves, as it contained an especially large proportion of the veteran members of that well-known corps. During the same hours of Tuesday a force of the Thirteenth Volunteer Heavy Artillery gathered at the Elm Street Armory, under the command of Colonel Howe, with three field-pieces ready for action.

Among the events of the night had been the capture and burning of the enrolment office at the corner of Grand and Ridge streets by the rioters in that section; but the deputy provost-marshal of that district, Captain Duffy, had already removed all papers, etc., to a place of safe-keeping, so that there, as elsewhere, the mob did not succeed in doing anything towards the "prevention of the Draft." Whoever occupied that and the adjoining buildings had to suffer, and a few innocent men were pounded; and that was all.

9

VIII.

Street to Street, House to House.

DURING the forenoon of Tuesday a segment of the mob worked very assiduously on First Avenue. Before twelve o'clock the area between Eleventh and Fourteenth streets was so heavily barricaded that it became a sort of fortified muster-ground for the rioters of that region. It so continued until that thoroughfare was at last reopened to public uses at a heavy cost of life and limb on the part of those who closed as well as of those who opened it. The neighboring telegraph-poles were cut down and laid across the avenue and the intersecting streets. Upon these were heaped carts, boxes, lumber, and rubbish, making barriers of a truly formidable description against anything short of artillery.

Near the locality of this barricade a couple of

large, patent street-sweeping machines which had been laid up over Sunday fell into the hands of the rabble. They were public property, and therefore lawful prize, and, what was more to the point, they were "labor-saving" machines; so they were burned amid ludicrously noisy expres-sions of mob-enmity to all that sort of thing.

The guards at the armories were now se-curely strong. That, for instance, at the Seventh Regiment Armory was maintained by four hun-dred men with two howitzers. A detachment of one hundred men of the Invalid Corps, with a serviceable force of sailors and marines, was posted in Worth Street near Broadway. A strong guard, with a battery, was posted at the Sub-Treasury, under command of Colonel Bliss of the Volunteers. Numerous other details of men were made by General Sandford for the protec-tion of important or exposed points and buildings. Lessons of wisdom as to such matters were being rapidly given. The residence of Colonel Robert Nugent, Deputy Provost-Marshal-General, had been sacked and burned before breakfast-time. At an earlier hour the bridge over McComb's Dam, Harlem River, had been burned. The "Washington Hall" hotel and building in Har-

lem had been plundered and burned by the sai
gang of marauders who had taken vengeance up
Colonel Nugent. They proceeded thence to
large planing-mill at One Hundred and Twen
ninth Street, and burned it down, with seve
buildings adjoining. It was difficult for a m
of sound mind to forecast what would be t
next freak of so much destructive insanity. E
dently the disorder was increasing rather th
diminishing, and there was need for all the m
who could be obtained; and how rapidly succe
ful were the recruiting processes may be in p
gathered from the fact that on Thursday, t
16th, the police commissariat was straining
resources to provide rations for about four thc
sand men. This, too, while the militia were c
ing for themselves to a great extent, and hot
and private citizens generally were exceeding
liberal in doing that sort of duty by the vario
bodies of men who were defending them.

The prevailing tone of the better part of t
public press may be taken from one sentence
an editorial article of the *Daily Times* of Tu
day morning. It was printed in italics:

" Crush the mob at once."

It was the right thing to say or do, and there were Gatling guns in the hallways of the *Times* building, and there were military and police drawn up in front of its barricaded windows. Other newspaper buildings were similarly guarded, and the wide-mouthed howitzer at the *Tribune* office corner, near by, was in charge of a detachment of United States seamen under command of Midshipman Stephen D. Adams.

The number of "special policemen" actually accepted and sworn in was already large, and before sunset swelled to about twelve hundred; but the military forces were gathered at so many places and under so many different and semi-independent commanders that no sort of estimate could be made of their number or availability. President Acton was compelled to obtain from them such assistance as he could and as best he might, with a very indefinite idea of what it might prove to be in any given case, however loyally and eagerly tendered. He had General Brown with him for counsel at the Central Office, and under his immediate direction were three companies of United States regular troops, numbering about one hundred and fifty, thoroughly trustworthy and well commanded. Of . these, maintained at that number by successive "reliefs," Mr. Acton made excellent use from the beginning to the end, and they finely illustrated the advantage possessed by disciplined valor over any mob.

The forenoon of Tuesday was one of constantly-increasing preparation and power on both sides of the great struggle. The mob was manifestly infuriated rather than awed, as yet, by the resistance it had met with, and it broke forth into more and more atrocious cruelties and daring outrages with each succeeding hour.

There were rumors, as there had been during the previous day, of an intended raid upon the Navy Yard in Brooklyn. The amount of government property there was enormous, and the yard was depleted of its ordinarily moderate garrison of marines, for these had been sent to fight the mob in the streets of New York. The workmen there employed were a respectable set of men, but they were unorganized, and it was not known how far they could be trusted as fighting material in case of an attack. They had not been hired as riflemen but as mechanics, and there were signs of trepidation among them. It

is likely that they could have been readily induced to fight, but no such effort was made, and
probably none was needed. The likelihood of
an attack was reduced to zero by the naval commanders. All the approaches to the yard were
put under cover of the guns of the receiving-
ship "North Carolina," of forty guns; the cor-
vette "Savannah," of twenty-two guns ; and of
the steam gun-boats "Granite City," "Gertrude,"
"Unadilla," eight guns each, and "Tulip," of six
guns. The precautions taken at this point were
unmistakably ample ; and at the same time the
iron-clad battery "Passaic" and the steam gunboat "Fuchsia" took up good positions off the old
Battery, at the southern extremity of New York,
to interfere with any mischievous expedition to
Governor's Island in the absence of its garrison.
None of the marauding bands of the mob were
likely to trust themselves upon the water under
such circumstances, and their hands were getting
very full upon the land.

President Acton was still toiling under moun-
tainous difficulties, but he was busily striking
hard blows at every available point or opportunity. Several hard fights were in progress at one
and the same hour, with any number of minor

collisions between the everywhere rising rioters and their multiplying antagonists. At 8.30 o'clock came word from the Twenty-first Precinct :

"A large mob is collecting on Second Avenue and Thirty-fourth Street, and threatening to burn all property in that vicinity."

More and more clearly, as the riot went on, did it assume and declare its true character as an "anti-property mob," with a leadership and membership of thieves, murderers, and incendiaries, reckless alike of human rights and human suffering.

Reports came in rapidly from several precincts. From the Seventh at 8.30 :

"Everything is quiet, but the mob is congregating in the vicinity of South Street."

At five minutes past nine o'clock, from the Tenth Precinct :

"A large crowd has collected about the Hook. They were last seen going down Jackson Street."

"About Corlear's Hook" included some of the very worst elements of the city's population, and a crowd gathered there was a sure promise of mischief to come.

Five minutes later, from the Twentieth Precinct:

"Information has just been received that about two thousand men, armed with clubs and revolvers, left the corner of Thirty-first Street and Tenth Avenue and marched down town. The intelligence is brought by Captain of Police S. Carpenter."

The "West Side" of the city was fast imitating the "East Side," and some of the hardest of Tuesday's fighting was done in districts commonly regarded as respectable.

The mob in the Twenty-first Precinct, as on Monday, was peculiarly desperate. At quarter past nine o'clock President Acton telegraphed his faithful lieutenants there:

"Is everything all right?"

and was answered:

"No. Far from it. The mob have burned one or two buildings on Second Avenue and Thirty-fourth Street."

The extent of the trouble brewing in that locality was quickly understood, and that it required sharp treatment was evident. Stages had been "impressed" freely in which to transport the police more rapidly and with less fatigue from one post of duty to another, securing greater efficiency and preventing a needless exhaustion of men at hard work in such hot weather. Few questions had been asked of either the drivers or owners of those stages. The former received a fair warning from the prompt locking-up of the first man who refused to drive.

Into omnibus after omnibus Inspector Carpenner hurried about three hundred Metropolitans, and set off at speed for Second Avenue. At a reasonable nearness to the scene of intended action the force dismounted, formed, and went forward. At ten minutes before ten o'clock President Acton telegraphed the Twenty-first Precinct:

"How is it now?"

and the instant answer came:

"Wait a few minutes—"

and then, a little afterwards:

"The force has arrived, and we are giving it to them. Shots are fired—"

There were reasons for the sudden breaking-off

of that response. The Inspector found such a mob before him as he had never yet confronted, but he charged them at the head of his men with his accustomed audacity. Every inch was fought for, desperately, between Thirty-fourth and Thirty-fifth streets, and the Metropolitans found their enemies closing in upon their rear. At the same moment they were assailed by showers of missiles from the houses on either side, all of which appeared to have been captured and occupied by the excited rioters. It was a complete trap, set and baited with cunning calculation. The situation of the police seemed critical in the extreme. Had they yielded or been overpowered, their fate at the hands of their enemies would have been one mournful to contemplate. Momentarily they wavered and staggered under the sudden pressure; but it was only for a moment. They were fighting for life, and they rallied. They fought their way on up the avenue and out of the trap. They then turned upon the mob and charged again, scattering it and filling the gutters with disabled ruffians. That done, they chased the fugitives into and through the houses and out upon the roofs, throwing them downstairs to be dealt with by other clubs below. More than one desperate rioter lost his footing on the slopes and edges of those roofs and came crashing down upon the pavements below. A four-story building is a bad place to fall from. Hard blows, however, had genuine mercy in them, and anything less than victory was cruelty to the mob itself and to the entire community. A number of ruffians still held Riley's porter-house, on the corner of Thirty-fourth Street, barring the doors and windows and defying assault. The police broke in the barricaded doors and "stormed the fort." The roughs were pitched out into the street, and Inspector Carpenter led his men on up the avenue. They were met, shortly, by a detachment of the Eleventh New York Volunteers, under Colonel O'Brien. This was the colonel's own regiment, and he had tendered the services of himself and men to the city. He was accompanied by an artillery force under Lieutenant Eagleson, with two field-pieces.

Thus strengthened, Inspector Carpenter wheeled around to make another attempt to clear the avenue thoroughly. Near the former battleground, the infuriated mob had rallied to meet them and attacked at once. The cannon were fired with blank cartridges only, although the

rioters were not firing "blanks;" but the volunteers under O'Brien used ball-cartridges at once.
Their volley killed seven and wounded many more,
and the shattered throng broke and fled at once,
vowing vengeance upon O'Brien and his men.
They fulfilled their threats terribly, as to him,
only a few hours later. For the time being, the
Second Avenue gathering was pretty well broken
up; but as soon as the police and military were
out of sight it reappeared, in a more bitter and
vindictive state of mind than ever.

Precisely at the time of the beginning of this
battle, 10 o'clock A.M., others were going on.
In Delancey Street a company of United States
regular troops, under Lieutenant Wood, was assailed and surrounded by a dense mob, and fired
repeated volleys at close quarters into the densely-
packed and yelling crowd, dispersing them for the
time being. The number of killed and wounded
was not ascertained. About half an hour later
the same company was again surrounded and hard
pressed in Pitt Street, and again fired rapidly,
with similar results. The mob returned, after the
passage of the military, and cared for their own
dead and wounded. There are no recorded estimates of the casualties on either side.

Shortly after sending off Inspector Carpenter and his force, Mr. Acton set out upon a tour of personal observation. It was not the most prudent thing to do, but it gave him a better idea of what was going on. At quarter past ten o'clock he telegraphed to the Central Office from his place "in the field:"

"Notify General Sandford to send the military to the Thirteenth Ward. There is an attack on houses in Goerck Street."

At 10.35 the Thirteenth Precinct telegraphed:

"Send military here immediately."

And ten minutes later Mr. Acton sent another despatch, to the Seventh Precinct:

"Find military and send them to the Thirteenth forthwith."

The trouble in that part of the city began at an early hour, as already recorded, and the gathering of the rabble "about the Hook" had been ominous for evil. To an inquiring despatch, a little later, "How are things now?" it was replied:

"There is a large mob at foot of Broome Street. No force arrived yet."

And again, at 10.55:

" Delamater Iron Works threatened by a crowd collected at the foot of Fourteenth Street."

It looked as if the manufacture of steam-boilers was in some inscrutable way to be connected with the Draft Act.

A force was on its way, and one of its intended supports was a company of marines arriving from the Navy Yard.

At 10.40 o'clock the Thirteenth Precinct reported :

" The mob came in contact with the marines in Delancey Street. The marines fired into them, hurting quite a number."

The rioters were to learn rapidly and terribly the effect to be produced upon a dense pack of men by rifle-work at short range from well-drilled and steady men, firing either by platoons or " file-firing." They were also speedily to receive ideas as to the consequences of facing repeated discharges of grape and canister from field-guns and howitzers at close quarters.

At 11.35 the Thirteenth Precinct was asked, " Anything new?" and could only answer :

" Great excitement.   Several killed and wounded."

How many, even aproximately, could not well be ascertained ; for the ground the brief skirmish was fought upon was almost immediately again in possession of the mob, while the police and military were in no condition to carry off either dead or wounded of their enemies.   They had as much as they could do to care for their own and for themselves.

At 10.50 A.M. the Sixteenth Precinct reported:

" All the stores are closing on Eighth Avenue, from fear of the mob in Seventeenth Street.'

And President Acton at once telegraphed to the Twentieth Precinct :

" Tell General Sandford to send a force to Seventeenth Street and Eighth Avenue."

The renewed fighting in the Twenty-first Precinct was now assuming wider and more threatening proportions.   Well was it for the Metropolitans that their reinforcements were coming forward so liberally.   Their own conduct was calling forth golden opinions from all competent observers.   General Harvey Brown was no novice in any kind of warfare.   He was now at the

Central Office, and keenly watched the swift transaction of its business, giving its chief his most
vigorous co-operation. He enthusiastically declared of the Metropolitans, "I never saw such
drill and discipline in all my life, and I was born
in the Army."

In response to an inquiry from him as to the
advisability of serving out muskets to the force,
Mr. Acton sensibly replied: "They are thoroughly
drilled to the use of the club, but would be raw
troops with rifles. It would only turn them from
good police into poor militia. They can do their
best work with the weapons they are trained to."

The soundness of this decision was well sustained in all the terrible hand-to-hand struggles
of the riot; but it must in justice be added that
every policeman was also well drilled in the use of
the revolver, was armed with a good one, and
that he employed it with excellent effect. It
came into play more and more frequently as the
fight proceeded.

At 10.40 A.M. the Twenty-first Precinct reported, in reply to Mr. Acton's question of
"What news?"—

"The military are shooting. Minié balls. Just flew
past this street. Blank cartridges in cannons only. This
10

force is clearing the streets, but the mob gathers quickly at other points. Several of mob killed and badly wounded. We have the best of the fight."

It was going forward in several parts of the precinct at once, and different bodies of military were at work, besides that with Inspector Carpenter on Second Avenue; but no record was kept by any officer. All that plainly appears is the general idea that the rioters got very much the worst of it in killed and wounded, and yet that their opponents only held a part of the ground at the end of it all. "Blank cartridges in cannons only" were fired only at the beginning; but soon the cannoneers were forced to resort to grape and canister, if but to prevent the mob from getting possession of the guns, ammunition and all. It was no time for vacillation. Fifteen minutes later, or at five minutes before eleven o'clock, it was necessary for General Brown to telegraph to the Twentieth Precinct:

"Send to the Arsenal. Say: A heavy battle is going on. Captain Wilkins' company of regulars will report to me here at once.

(Signed)   "HARVEY BROWN,
               "*Brigadier-General Commanding.*"

More help was arriving, for at eleven o'clock precisely came a despatch from the Eleventh Precinct:

" A company of marines just reported here., Have you any instructions?"

The new-comers were speedily given enough to do, for there were calls for assistance from many different directions. The Sixteenth Precinct sent word at 11.18 o'clock:

" Report says mob is coming to station-house. Will have no men."

The Eighteenth Precinct telegraphed:

" The mob is very wild on the corner of Twenty-second Street and Second Avenue."

And added, at 11.22:

" I don't know but I will have to leave."

The Central Office itself was almost bare of protection, and a despatch was sent to the Twenty-first Precinct at 11.38:

" Can you send a few men here?"

The answer was:

" We have three sections guarding the station, which is threatened. It is unsafe for men to be seen in uniform. Consequently they have their uniforms put away. Shall I send them ?"

The peril indicated did not affect the Metropolitans as a body, for the men in the fights were almost all in uniform. No small squad, however, in that manner marked for destruction, could have made its way through the mob-governed areas around the Central Office, or through any other considerable part of the city. Any kind of uniform, including an obtrusively expensive suit of clothes, was supposed to indicate a supporter of law and its authorities, and was an offence subjecting the wearer to the death-penalty at the hands of Crime and its authorities.

Things were now getting into something like working order. On assuming command, on Monday, General Brown had at once telegraphed from the Central Office, through the Twentieth Precinct :

" *To Major-General Sandford, at Arsenal :*

" I am in command of the United States troops in the city. Order the commanders of those with you to report to me.

(Signed)   " HARVEY BROWN, *Brigadier General.*"

The forenoon of Tuesday closed hotly in the Eighteenth Precinct. At 11.20 o'clock the men at that station-house telegraphed:

" What shall we do? The mob is about 450 strong."

The answer was instantaneous :

" Clean them down if you can. T. C. ACTON."

At 11.35 they again telegraphed :

" They have attacked the Union Steam Factory, **on the** corner of—"

There it stopped. Mr. Acton telegraphed to the Twentieth :

" Send another hundred men forthwith."

But it was just then a vain order, for lack of men ; and the works whose possession had been sharply contested were captured by the rioters.

At 11.35 it was asked of the Eighteenth :

" Is there any trouble at the foot of Twenty-sixth Street ?"

But the operator answered not for five minutes, and then his despatch had a sort of breathless expression :

" I must leave. The mob is here with guns."

With reference to the condition of the Eighteenth, Mr. Acton telegraphed to the Twentieth at 11.50 o'clock:

"Has that company started yet?"

And, after some explanation, he was informed:

"The company left a quarter of an hour ago."

When, therefore, at 12 o'clock, noon, the Eighteenth asked him anxiously, "Is relief coming?" he could say:

"They are on their way up. They will be there as soon as they can."

The reinforcements came in time to prevent immediate disaster, but only to postpone a final defeat at that point.

At 11.35 o'clock came a despatch from the Twentieth Precinct:

"Send one hundred men to disperse a crowd breaking windows in Mayor Opdyke's house."

Five minutes later, one from the Twenty-second Precinct said:

"The mob has gone to Mr. Higgins's carpet factory, at foot of Forty-third Street, to burn it."

This was no isolated case, although a great many such undertakings were frustrated by the timely interference of the police and soldiery. Any factory, of any trade, the workmen of which refused to become rioters was an object of mob execration, and was to be destroyed if possible. A large proportion of such establishments did not open for work until order was restored, and some of those whose "hands" were sufficiently numerous and determined took efficient measures for self-protection, the workmen declaring their readiness to use fire-arms rather than be driven from their rights or recruited into the ranks of crime.

The more intelligent part of the mob was well aware how important to them was the continued absence of the militia regiments. They knew, vaguely, that there was a danger of a return of some of these, at some time, or of the arrival from the interior of the State of armed reinforcements for the authorities. The Hudson River counties were as completely denuded of troops as the city itself, and no such forces had been sent for by the Governor. Nevertheless, at half-past eleven o'clock, the Twentieth Precinct reported:

" A mob tearing up the track on Eleventh Avenue."

This was the track, or one of the several tracks, of the New York Central and Hudson River Railroad.   Cars full of soldiery might roll into the city over it; and if the end of it should be torn off, where would they roll to, indeed?   There is nothing left of a railroad, once you have cut off the end of it and disconnected it with you. Something or other in their heads prevented the rioters from perceiving the futility of all their hard work.   They appear not even to have known the topography of their adopted city. Soldiers could have been landed from a train of cars at any point north of that " break" and have quietly marched the rest of their way into the city, or they could have been landed from steamers at any required point along the entire water-frontage.   President Acton's only reply was :

" Tell Sandford what they are doing."

That part of the field of battle was now almost entirely under military supervision.

Two minutes before noon the Thirteenth Precinct reported :

" The mob have just sacked a large gun-store in Grand Street, and are coming and on their way to attack us."

It was only too true ; and seven minutes later came from that point the news of the first defeat of the military by the mob :

" The marines have left us and gave way. They are hot here."

It looked like that; but Mr. Acton's reply was encouraging :

" We will send some more in a few minutes."

Noon had come. The mob was manifestly increasing in its proportions and activities, but it had gained no important advantages during the morning hours, while all the forces required for its rapid and sure suppression were steadily augmenting. President Acton felt and confidently declared that he could already see the beginning of the end ; but he also knew that he had yet a hard task before him, with abundant possibilities of disaster.

IX.

A Very Hot Afternoon.

THE Governor of the State of New York was informed on Monday, by telegraph, of the dangerous condition of affairs in the city. He arrived early on Tuesday, and proceeded to the headquarters of the Mayor, at the St. Nicholas Hotel.

There was no reason why the Governor should not accept, as he did, the prevailing idea that the riot was a violent reaction against the prolonged exactions of the National Government, occasioned by the Civil War, to which, and to the political party managing it, he was himself opposed. With his political views and relations, however, this story has nothing whatever to do. He was otherwise in a very embarrassing position. He was a gentleman of wealth, culture, and capacity, a lover of peace. He held the high and responsible position of Governor, and many men were looking to him for active measures. In any other part of the State he might have done much, but on Manhattan Island, for an especial reason, he could do almost nothing.

New York is not like other towns in some things. It has been Dutch, and it has been English, and it has been American, and there is no telling what it is now; but it has had more charters than any other living city. Its government is a puzzle made up of all its charters and all the legislation concerning them, supplemented by its relations, as a great, fortified seaport, to the National Government. In 1863, as now, it had its Mayor and Board of Aldermen. Also, it had a Board of Councilmen; and the *county* of New York, occupying precisely the same limits as the *city* of New York, had its Board of Supervisors. Then, however, as now, the greater part of the administrative functions provided for by law were intrusted to Boards of Commissioners. Over these the Mayor and Aldermen had little control; and some of them owed small allegiance to anybody.

Most powerful and most independent of all was the Board of Police Commissioners, ruling what was called " The Metropolitan Police District." This included the entire counties of New

York, Westchester, Richmond (Staten Island), with Kings and a part of Queens (on Long Island). Over all this region all police authority was vested by law in the Police Board, and they possessed sole power to call out and direct the local military forces, to order " firing," etc.   During the riot the Board did so call out the military.   All armed bodies of men who served did so under the Police Department, or actually without au- thority.   General Harvey Brown, commanding the United States troops, considered it his duty to be guided by the letter and spirit of the State law.   General Sandford, of the State militia, failed to do so or to report to the Police Department, except as will be hereafter stated.   Among minor commanders there was a general ignorance of the statutory provisions.   Many irregular activities are inevitable after chaos has obtained, and Presi- dent Acton sharply disapproved of the over-zeal of certain squads of men who, as he expressed it, " went a-gunning on their own account."

Had the law assigning the local uses of the militia been otherwise, Governor Seymour's pow- er was limited by the fact that he had already sent out of the State every regiment at his dis- posal.   By his direction, at the call of President

Lincoln, there had gone from the city of New York the Fourth, Sixth, Seventh, Eighth, Eleventh, Twelfth, Twenty - second, Thirty - fifth, Thirty-seventh, Sixty-ninth, and Seventy-first, and from Brooklyn the Thirteenth, Twenty-third, Twenty-eighth, Thirty-second, Forty-seventh, and Fifty-sixth.

The net result of all consultations was that there was very little within the immediate reach of the Governor. He addressed a large and fairly orderly assembly gathered in front of the City Hall, appealing to them as citizens, in behalf of law and order. He spoke again to a crowd of business men on Wall Street, and to another in the upper part of the city ; but his words did not reach the ears of many actual rioters. He prepared two proclamations, which were afterwards printed and will be found in the Appendix of this book. The Governor would have been very glad to put out the fire, but he had no way of getting at it. Besides, he was like a great many other very good men, blinded by political preoccupation and entirely at fault concerning the character and meaning of that mob. Consequently his visit was without perceptible use in restraining disorder.

The fighting was not interrupted for one moment, on Tuesday. Noon came, and still it went right on, at many widely-separated points. The Metropolitans were so busy with their own work that they made no attempt to keep track of or to report the operations of the military. They knew that bodies of soldiers were moving here and there with increasing numerical strength, and with widely-varying efficiency. The city's ordinary business was suspended. Only an affair of pressing importance would induce anybody to venture into the more disturbed regions, and people generally were disposed to keep within doors. Along the entire water-front, the long-shoremen and others who earned their bread by handling freight had been so thoroughly "notified" of the awful consequences of being found at work that they were no longer willing to take the risk. The lading and unlading of vessels had almost ceased. Commerce dies in the presence of Anarchy.

Here and there a steamer's wharf was under the guns of an armed vessel, or had other efficient protection, and its laborers toiled on in personal security.

The great eruption might now be considered at its height.

At the Police Headquarters the tide of warnings and appeals had swollen fast. From the outset the rioters had aimed at obtaining fire-arms. The several arsenals had been almost continually menaced. At 12.35 o'clock the Twentieth Precinct telegraphed:

"Send two hundred men forthwith to Thirty-fifth Street Arsenal."

One minute later came this from the Twenty-first Precinct:

" The mob have just broken open a gun-store in Third Avenue and are arming themselves. Between Thirty-sixth and Thirty-seventh streets."

They were doing the same sort of thing at other points. The Civil War had given a tremendous impulse to that branch of trade and manu-facture, and the dealers in arms were many times more numerous and kept heavier stocks on hand than was or is customary in days of peace ; but their supplies of ammunition, although considerable in the aggregate, were not permitted to be very large in any one place.

At other points the riot was flaring up into a sort of general conflagration. At 12.40 o'clock

this despatch came from the Twentieth Precinct :

" Allerton's Hotel on Eleventh Avenue is sacked and
burning."

This was done by the mob who were tearing
up the railroad track.

As on the previous day, the fighting in the
Twenty-first Precinct was severe and bloody.
Simultaneously with the news of the hotel-burn-
ing at 12.40, the Twenty-first reported :

" Send help.   The crowd is desperate."

The entire police force was already in the streets,
and ten minutes later the few men at that station-
house telegraphed :

" The mob is armed and we are unprotected."

All that Mr. Acton could reply was :

" We will send help as soon as possible."

The promised help was duly sent, and no immediate disaster was reported.

Frequent notices now came in of the " finding
of dead bodies."   These called for the services of

the coroner; but comparatively few formal inquests could be held, then or afterwards. Each
" finding" was itself a grisly comment upon the
inevitable results of anarchy.

At 12.45 o'clock General Sandford telegraphed
the Central Office :

" Colonel Nugent is requested to send me two hundred
good troops forthwith. The Arsenal is threatened. My
men are all out."

That telegram meant a good deal. Colonel
Nugent at that hour had only the Invalid Corps
detachment under his command, with hardly a
sound man in it, and the idea that he could send
" good troops" was almost grotesque in its absurdity ; but the demand of General Sandford presents
a truthful index of the state of military activity
already attained. The regulars controlled by
General Brown were at such work as had been
assigned them, and so were all naval details which
had arrived. The one thousand men reported
as ready for service at the Arsenal on Monday
evening had all been sent out, mostly to guard or
garrison duty, and so had any others gathered
within General Sandford's reach during the forenoon of Tuesday. The men collected at other

military rallying-points were distinctly not available or within his reach.   He may or may not have
been justified in regarding the Arsenal as seriously threatened, but the.force he had retained there
must have been small.   The fragmentary nature
of all the good or bad military and other material at this hour suggests more than one lesson.   The strength of the mob in the streets is
further illustrated by the fact already recorded,
that the Metropolitan Police, with now nearly
twelve hundred sworn " specials," were so occupied in facing it that a hotly-assailed station-house
called for help in vain.   There is now no possible
means of tracing the rapid events of such a hurly-
burly, even if it were desirable to do so.   That
which left no record must be estimated by the
sure indications given by ascertained facts correlated.

After some delay, Colonel Nugent was found,
and this answer was returned to the Twentieth
Precinct :

" For Wells, of Colonel Nugent's staff : Colonel Nugent
has no men for General Sandford.   Notify him.'

It was necessary that the men at the several
localities should be fed ; and the police commis-

sariat was ready with supplies, but was compelled
to transmit them as opportunities offered. Except
within very uncertain limits the streets of the city
were not available for transportation purposes,
but the North and East rivers had not been
barricaded. At ten minutes before one o'clock
this despatch went to the First Precinct :

"Send to police boat to take up provisions and bring
down five hundred men. T. C. ACTON."

This boat was not armed, but note should be
taken of its usefulness in effecting transfers of
men ; and also of the important protection given
the city along the water-front by the United
States armed vessels.

Here and there, in spite of all the storm and
confusion, a ray of human nature broke in amid
the increasing gloom of the Central Office telegrams. At 1.12 o'clock P.M. the following was
sent to the Fifth Precinct :

" Send to Dr. Purple, 183 Hudson Street, to go as soon
as possible to Inspector Leonard's house. Baby very
sick. '

The father was leading his men against a throng
of pitiless brigands, but the sick baby was not for-

gotten.   Seven minutes later this also went, through the Twentieth Precinct, on behalf of Inspector Carpenter:

"Notify Mrs. Carpenter I am all right."

That he was so is one of the many marvels of the survival of the men most frequently in deadly peril.   There were many inquiries at the Central Office and at the station-houses, during those days of tumult, from the anxious wives and children of policemen, but not many of them could at once be definitely answered.   There was nothing for it but to suffer and to wait.   Alas for the many to whom, at last, only sad news came after all their weary waiting!

The rush for weapons by the rioters continued. At eight minutes past one o'clock the Twentieth Precinct reported:

"A mob has begun to rifle gunsmiths in this precinct. Shall we not take possession of the arms in places not yet attacked?"

President Acton's opinion was adverse to this, for several reasons, and he answered:

"No.   If you want help we will send you a force."

Ten minutes later the Fourth Precinct also reported :

" We want more help to stop the riot. They are going to break open the gun-store in Catherine Street."

At 1.30 P.M. the Twentieth again announced :

" A mob are about burning up a large feed-store in Ninth Avenue near Twenty-ninth Street."

The leaders of the rabble were growing more ambitious, as they obtained possession of arms and ammunition and found themselves able to hold their opponents temporarily at bay. At three minutes past two o'clock the Twentieth Precinct reported :

" The mob is now taking the horses from the Red Bird Line stables, to organize a troop."

It is difficult to imagine a more ludicrous affair than such a " troop" would have been. Half-tipsy miscreants mounted upon omnibus-horses, and charging, without skill or drill, over the stone pavements of New York City !

The Seventh Precinct reported at 2.30 P.M. :

" There is a large crowd collected at the corner of Market and Monroe streets, and they have demolished a negro shanty in the rear. They number some five hundred, and they threaten to fire the premises."

Nothing could be done for that locality just then, for the battle in the Twenty-second Precinct was getting hotter and more doubtful, and at the same instant a telegram from that quarter reported :

"Military has arrived and fired on the mob corner Tenth Avenue and Forty-fourth Street."

The soldiers had not been sent in sufficient force, for only ten minutes later the news of the second notable disaster to the military arrived by way of the Twentieth Precinct :

"I hear the mob has defeated and dispersed the military. We have one of the wounded."

Alas for the poor wounded soldier whose hard fate threw him into the power of that brutal rabble ! Better for him to have been killed outright by his first hurt.

This was at 2.40 P.M.; and ten minutes later the Twentieth Precinct was obliged to ask on its own account :

"We expect to be attacked. Shall we fight to the bitter end ?"

They received the laconic reply:

" Fight. ACTON."

The resistance made was temporarily successful, and the operator at that station-house sent
word in a quarter of an hour, at 3.05 P.M. :

" Captain Walling says he has had a fight and whipped
them, corner of Fifth Avenue and Forty-seventh Street.
He wants more men, if they can be spared. If not, he
says, send word if he shall return. Send the reinforcements to this station."

Fresh orders were sent, and the reinforcements
with them, but the mob was gathering faster and
fiercer. At 4.25 P.M. a message reached the Sixteenth Precinct station-house to send word to
the Central Office :

" Just left the Twentieth. Excitement awful. They
had to clear out the military on the ground, and the mob
was about to make for the station-house."

The repulsed soldiery speedily recovered their
lost ground, and the rioters were driven in their
turn, with heavy losses, but the hard-worked
Metropolitans were given only a brief breathing
spell.

President Acton's attention followed all the movements of his foes with steady vigilance. At 3.25 P.M. he sent to the Sixth Precinct:

" Look out for Baxter Street. The mob are going to fire some negro dwellings."

Beyond a doubt the mob supposed its cruel cowardice especially opposed to the War for the Union. One of its insane fragments marched, in the course of Tuesday afternoon, to the hospital on Forty-first Street near Lexington Avenue, with the avowed purpose of burning it. Their only assigned or assignable reason for a deed so peculiarly hellish was that the hospital contained about two hundred and fifty wounded Union soldiers. The cardinal sin of these men was that they had dared to suffer for the country which their would-be destroyers had invaded by way of the immigrant station at Castle Garden. It was a sin requiring that they should be burned alive if possible.

The gathered executioners were met and repulsed, after a moderately sharp fight, by a force of armed citizens, and the hospital was rescued.

Another detachment of the mob marched that afternoon to the Columbia College property, with the loudly declared intention of burning the buildings. They had no reason for connecting these with the government or the Draft, although President King and others of the faculty were well known as patriotic citizens. The truth of the matter was that all such institutions were an obvious and offensive product of the social order and civilization against which that mob was a rebellion.

The crowd were not altogether settled in their views and convictions. They were met upon the college grounds by a Roman Catholic priest, who boldly confronted them and addressed them so convincingly that he succeeded in diverting them from their purpose. His name is not reported, but his courage and eloquence achieved a memorable triumph.

During all of Tuesday forenoon the mob retained a hotly-disputed possession of their old battle-ground on Second Avenue above Twentieth Street. Here were the yet smoking ruins of the Twenty-first Street Armory, and here, on the corner above, was the Union Steam Works, or "wire factory," containing about four thousand carbines. Not only had the mob driven the police from this building, but they had even

undertaken to garrison it and hold it :
headquarters.   It was probably due 1
tastic idea in the minds of leading riot
the carbines and rifles stored in the fz
not immediately carried off.   They we,
rily reserved for more judicious distril
only a part had been given out to
were intended to use them.

At ten o'clock Inspector George W
ordered to take command of about tw
Metropolitans, clear Second Avenue
ture the "wire factory," as it was
from its former uses.   He marche
through Twenty-first Street into the av
ing the mob in the centre.   The exci
greeted him and his moderate force w
of derision, and his position was ful
and danger.   To attack was hazard
extreme, but to retreat might have
so.   The rioters in the factory at once
removal of the guns on notice that
were at hand.   Inspector Dilks did nc
for a moment, and the fight which
brought out and tested to the utte
thorough training of the men under his
It was a charge in close order, penetra

ily the infuriated multitude that fought hard for every inch of ground, and then a long, hand-to-hand struggle for very life, in front of the factory, until the mob in the street, discouraged by severe handling and terrible clubbing, broke and fled, leaving most of its plunder behind it. The pavement of the avenue was thickly strewn with bleeding and disabled men. Many of the police had been hurt, and some badly, but none were killed.

The factory was still densely garrisoned by the rioters, and a most determined resistance was made against the attack of the Metropolitans.

The entrance was forced and the interior was won, inch by inch, by desperate, hand-to-hand fighting. Some idea of its severity is to be obtained from the professional report of a single physician who dressed the wounds of some of the rioters. He cared for twenty-one wounds "in the head" alone, all made by the locust club, and all fatal. What was the aggregate of hurts of other kinds or dressed by other physicians can only be surmised.

The recaptured weapons were heaped upon a large express-wagon as high as they could be piled. Each policeman took what he could carry, and the command marched back towards the Central Office. It was returning from a well-won victory, and the people poured out of the houses along the way to cheer the triumphal procession enthusiastically. The hearts of all decent citizens were with the Metropolitans that day, and Dilks and his men and their trophies were a sort of sunshine in a great darkness.

The capture of the factory was accomplished by about 2 o'clock P.M., and the command reached the Central Office at about 3 o'clock, deeming their work secure. But it was an over-hasty conclusion. Only a few men had been left in charge of the building, and Captain Helm had been ordered to proceed, with some of the Eighteenth Precinct police, and remove a lot of carbines which had been left behind. At about half-past three o'clock word came to the Central Office that there was worse trouble than ever at the "wire factory;" and it was only too true, for the furiously exasperated rioters had gathered in greater numbers and with even a deadlier determination. Inspector Dilks marched again, with two hundred Metropolitans and a company of regular infantry under Captain Franklin. Second Avenue was entered through Twenty-first Street, as before, only just in time to rescue Captain Helm and his men from being overpowered by numbers. The fight which followed was fierce but brief, and the building and the remaining arms were secured. It was now deemed advisable to "clear the neighborhood," and a march began with the soldiery in front and the Metropolitans acting as rearguard and as skirmishers on the flanks, paying attention to the houses from which missiles were thrown or fired. The route ordered was through Twenty-second Street into First Avenue, and one man was killed, at a window on the way, in the very act of hurling down a heavy "rock" upon the heads of the police. As the force wheeled into First Avenue it was fiercely assailed, and Captain Franklin ordered the rioters to disperse or he should fire. He was answered by shouts of derision and showers of paving-stones. There was no help for it, and several volleys were fired in rapid succession, with terrible effect. The forces moved steadily forward, down the avenue, the soldiers firing on the mob as they went, while the police attended to the fusillade from the houses. At Twenty-first Street the mob broke and scattered, and the Inspector ordered a counter-march to and through Twenty-second Street to Second Avenue again. The neigborhood was not even then cleared, for the rioters were again in strength at the corner of Second Avenue and Twenty-first Street, and began another attack which called for repeated volleys. The march through other streets and back to the Central Office was little molested after that, but the rioters in due time again took possession of the now emptied factory and burned it to the ground.

Towards noon of Tuesday a detachment of the west-side mob marched down Sixth Avenue, forcibly recruiting its ranks as it went, avowing its intention of " burning No. 37," the residence of a prominent Republican politician. His political opinions marked him out as a proper person to be murdered and to have his property destroyed, for there is no other despotism comparable to the blind tyranny of a mob. The rioters were met and driven by the police of the Twentieth Precinct and a company of regulars under Captain Putnam. Repeatedly broken, they rallied again and again, as they were pushed along up the avenue. They at last turned through one of the cross streets, and were followed into Fifth Avenue. Here they undertook to make a final stand, but were scattered by a bayonet-charge, the locust clubs plying industriously on them, at the flanks of the advancing line of leveled steel. Not a shot was fired, but the pavement was strewn with disabled rioters.

Towards the close of the afternoon the rioters in Pitt Street and Delancey Street renewed their assaults upon the dwellings of colored people. A detachment of U. S. marines was sent, with orders to "reopen those streets," and was surrounded precisely as the regulars had been in the morning. The marines were ordered to "fire low," and did so, killing twelve and wounding many more; but repeated volleys were not called for. That particular part of the riot had now received lessons enough as to the effect of musketry, and it scattered and did no rallying until after the marines had departed.

Among the almost innumerable minor incidents of the afternoon was a cowardly attack upon a public school-house in the Sixteenth Ward because a couple of colored women whom a mob was pursuing had taken refuge there. The teachers and scholars took courage of sheer fright, and barricaded the doors and windows so strongly as to keep their assailants at bay until help came. During the delay the marauders consoled themselves by demolishing a small house opposite the school because somebody said it was an abode of colored people.

In the course of Tuesday's fighting, while leading his men, Colonel O'Brien was hurt in one knee by a stone, but he continued to perform his duties until late in the afternoon. His residence was on Second Avenue, between Thirty-fourth and Thirty-fifth streets, and his family had already been removed from it to a place of greater safety. After their departure, which had been none too quickly made, the dwelling had been thoroughly sacked by the rioters.

The crowds which had filled Second Avenue were understood to have been effectually dispersed, and Colonel O'Brien desired to visit his home and ascertain the condition of affairs. It was a hazardous undertaking and should have been accompanied by a well-armed force; but a brave man does not always act with prudence. The Colonel went in a carriage, and, leaving it at Thirty-fifth

Street, proceeded to his own door on foot. He had evidently been waited for, but accounts vary as to the precise manner of his capture by his enemies. It was made upon his own threshold, at all events, and he fought for his life. He was overpowered by numbers, dragged out into his dooryard, and beaten cruelly. He was then dragged by the hair of his head out into the street, and pounded and tortured with fiendish malice. Both males and females took part in the brutal transaction. He was left lying upon the hot flagstones, dying of many hurts and panting with thirst. A humane man who kept a drug-store on the next corner dared to bring him a glass of water, but he paid dearly for so obeying the law of Christ. His life was spared, strangely enough, but his store was immediately sacked and gutted. Horrified men and women, looking from neighboring windows, were unable to refrain from expressing their indignation, and were answered by ferocious shouts of " Kill them, too. Don't let's have any witnesses;" but nothing was actu-ally done to them at the time. The dying man was left in his agony. Help arrived too late, and he was carried into a house that he might die more comfortably; but the bitterness of the mob forbade such an ending.   At nightfall they came again, and their victim was dragged forth.   A daring priest of the Catholic Church broke through the ring around him, and with difficulty obtained leave to administer the last rites of his religion. Breath left the body, and the courageous priest went for another like himself, and they two lifted the battered corpse upon a hand-barrow and carried it to Bellevue Hospital.   That was not all. The entire block of buildings contained human beings who had dared rebuke such awful inhumanity.   The mob was not quite prepared, as yet, to massacre so many men and women and children.   They lacked the courage if not the will for that; but they burned down every house in the entire row, with its contents, that all the householders of New York City might be taught better than openly to disapprove of murder.

The reason of an especial bitterness exhibited towards the Twentieth Precinct station-house appears in a despatch from the Sixteenth Precinct which reached the Central Office at 4.20 o'clock P.M :

" Colored children are now at Twentieth, and the crowd say they are coming to sack the building."

A throng of helpless little orphans was quite enough to provoke the ferocity of these wolves from the worst dens of Europe. The fact that the little ones were black of skin made it a crime to shelter them, even after their own pleasant home had been burned to the ground. It is positively comforting to know that the Metropolitans "hit hard" and that the soldiers "fired low" in repelling that particular attack, which was thoroughly done. So completely was the mob shattered and repulsed that when, at five o'clock, the Sixteenth Precinct reported:

"Large mob collected in Fifteenth Street and Seventh Avenue. I am looking for an attack on station-house any moment, and am alone "—

it was possible to answer:

"Send to Twentieth for assistance.   T. C. ACTON."

It was sent for, and it came; but it did not arrive any too soon, as several telegrams testify. One of these informed Mr. Acton:

"They are mobbing Sinclair's house, of *Tribune.* We have no force to send there."

He replied :

" Will send force in few minutes."

Incendiarism and robbery began to break out more and more viciously, as the eventful day drew near its close, but no reports came in of the many minor incidents. At 5.40 o'clock the Twenty-first Precinct reported :

" The mob are firing and breaking open stores on Third Avenue and Second Avenue near Fortieth Street."

But this was a sort of wholesale business.

At ten minutes past six o'clock the same precinct sent word of a yet more fiendish piece of revengeful destructiveness, the net results of which have already been given, but which carries with it a vivid presentation of the position of the entire field. The despatch read :

" A block of buildings near Thirty-fourth Street and Second Avenue will be attacked. It is where Colonel O'Brien lives. He is nearly beaten to death, and they are watching him that he may not recover."

Twenty minutes later the Twenty-first Precinct repeated its warning :

"Occupants of the entire block between Thirty-fourth and Thirty-fifth streets have been notified by the mob that they intend to fire it at dark."

There was no hesitation or delay in the fulfilment of the barbarous threat, for in five minutes more came the curt assurance:

" They have fired the block."

The buildings were plundered as well as burned, and the Colonel died upon the pavement, as has been related. The absence of cause or excuse for the action of the mob does not require to be enlarged upon. The fact, however, that the coming of such an affair was well known beforehand to the authorities, and that they were powerless to prevent it, throws a strong and lurid light upon the condition of New York City at sunset of the second day of the riot. That part of it wherein this deed was done had been "cleared" again and again, but was yet actually under control of the rabble. So exacting and exhausting were the demands of the general struggle at that hour that not one sufficiently strong detachment of police or of soldiers could Mr. Acton draw from the duty upon which it was engaged even to rescue a whole block of buildings from destruction. There may have been unoccupied forces here and there; but if so, they were not yet sufficiently "in hand," or were otherwise unavailable for such a fight as this would have been.

It is now impossible to ascertain with any accuracy the localities or the operations of the greater number of the detachments sent out by General Sandford, or nominally acting under him, during the afternoon of Tuesday. None seem to have made written reports to anybody, then or afterwards. A very large force was necessarily employed in "garrison duty," as the points and places directly or indirectly threatened by the mob were numerous; and so were those which required to be occupied and guarded, whether threatened or not. The volunteers were gathering with commendable zeal at the several mustering-places, but were for the greater part imperfectly organized. Prudence required that they should be put into shape somewhat before being exposed to the trying service before them of battling with superior numbers at close quarters. They could relieve the police and the detachments under General Brown of garrison duty, but as yet they could do but little more, with the exception of such fragments of old regiments, volunteer and militia, as could fall into line under their accustomed commanders.

Before 7 o'clock P.M. over twelve hundred " special policemen" had been duly enlisted and sworn in and armed, and many of these took an active share in street-fighting; but they could not be depended upon like the carefully drilled and trained Metropolitans.

President Acton passed a toilsome and anxious day, but he was as full of energy and confidence as ever. At ten minutes before 7 o'clock P.M. he telegraphed the Twentieth Precinct:

" Is General Sandford at Thirty-fifth Street Arsenal? If he is, ascertain what he is doing, and what assistance we can render him."

An answer came in half an hour:

" Sandford is not there. The military have returned, and Nugent says he has enough to hold the Arsenal."

At about the same time despatches informed the Central Office that the part of the Colored Orphan Asylum spared by the previous day's fire had again been kindled, but there was little that could be done in that direction. At five minutes before nine o'clock another message came from the Twentieth Precinct, and is a sort of telegraphic window through which a general view of the situation can be taken :

" In response to a former despatch, Sandford says he deems himself sufficiently strong.   If he should want assistance, he will send word through this station."

General Sandford's too frequently expressed conviction that he could hold the Arsenal, and that " all was quiet" there, had by this time supplied the Metropolitans with a standing joke, somewhat maliciously embodied in Mr. Acton's inquiry. Nevertheless the truth remains that the closing hours of Tuesday found the defenders of law and order " on guard." They were soberly confident of the result, but not by any means masters of the situation, though deeming themselves strong enough to hold their own through the night. The mob, however, held large parts of the city at their mercy, and had as yet no idea that they were in sure process of being " put down." They and their leaders were preparing for even more desperate and destructive work, and for a more severe and terrible punishment, before yielding.

At 7.40 P.M. General Brown sent this despatch through the Twenty-sixth Precinct :

‘ *To Major-General Sandford, at Arsenal:*
" I am in command of the U. S. troops in the city. Will you come to this office to consult with me ?
(Signed)   " HARVEY BROWN, *Brigadier-General.*"

At the same time he sent the following:

" *To Colonel Nugent :*
" I am in command of the U. S. troops in the city. Order the commanders of those with you to report to me.
(Signed)   " HARVEY BROWN, *Brigadier-General.*’

Active and intelligent co-operation could be obtained only by mutual consultation, and there seems to have been no positive working at cross-purposes.

.   There had been quite a number of public meetings in the course of the day, besides those addressed by Governor Seymour. One of merchants and bankers, irrespective of party lines, gathered at the Exchange Sales-room, No. 111 Broadway. Many speeches were made, and the tone of them all was to the last degree energetic and uncompromising. Resolutions were adopted and measures taken in furtherance of the various

organizations of armed citizens. The list closed
with a resolution calling for the immediate declaration of martial law ; but all men were quickly
to learn that there was no need of that. Other
meetings, at the Stock Exchange, Produce Exchange, and like centres of trade and commerce,
were similar in spirit and action ; and so were the
gatherings continuously held at the Union
League Club and in the parlors of the larger hotels ; and so, above all, were the growing "public meetings" at the armories.

X.

Through a Dark Night.

AT sunset of Tuesday the situation had many features that were perplexing and apparently discouraging. Among these was the disordered, interrupted condition of the entire telegraph service. Continuous and trustworthy intercommunication could not be had by either police or military. The station-houses, the armories, the arsenals, all the other posts held, were, with variations, so many detached garrisons. Bodies of the enemy, of unknown strength and purpose, were operating almost at will through all the intervening spaces. The streets and avenues served the rioters, to some extent, as so many " covered-ways."

The United States regular troops, under General Brown, were in close relations with Police Headquarters, and President Acton always knew where they were and what they were doing.

Of all " garrisoned posts" and their condition he could keep himself well advised. He had sent out numbers of detectives and other "spies" among the mob in every quarter of the city, and the reports of these men and of his efficient subordinates were pouring in continuously. There could hardly be any large gathering of sedition which did not now contain some of his operatives; but it was not easy for these to form a sound opinion as to what mischief was next to come.

As for the large amount of independent and unreported military action undertaken, some of it resulted disastrously, but on the whole it afforded valuable co-operation. It was work done for the common purpose and against the public enemy, whether it was done altogether wisely and well or not.

That was a heated, excited, bewildered time, of blind confusions and of sudden rushes hither and thither. So well was this understood that, even after all was over, neither the National Government, nor the State, nor the City demanded of any public servant a detailed report of the extraordinary occurrences of the week. Only through a prolonged and tedious search and careful analysis of miscellaneous and frequently conflicting data has it been possible to approximately ascertain the facts. The police and military were making very shrewd calculations, throughout, as to each other's doings. The citizens generally were within their own bolted doors and knew nothing of what might be going on beyond their immediate neighborhoods, and, as a rule, knew but little accurately of even that. The press reporters pursued their duties under insuperable difficulties. In several instances they narrowly escaped being murdered on discovery. From beginning to end of the disturbances the public press hesitated to print even what they thought they knew. As a rule they were reasonably careful to avoid sensational statements or the printing of rumors as facts. Various motives influenced all sorts of writers to a course which tended to prevent a needless increase of the excitement. An adequate journalistic picture of current events could neither be obtained nor given.

The evening began with a storm of telegrams to the Central Office.

At ten minutes past six o'clock the Twenty-first Precinct, West Thirty-fifth Street, the scene of so much hard fighting already, sent warning:

" The mob in strong force threatens to make an attack upon us here to-night.   Help us if you can."

Help was scarce at that hour, but Mr. Acton cheerfully responded :

" A force is at Sixteenth.   When they settle with mob they will come and help you."

At 6.15 o'clock a telegram arrived from the Twenty-seventh Precinct :

" There is a colored boy at Mrs. Hanan's, 45 Greenwich Street, and she tells me they have threatened to burn the place unless she sends him away.   What shall be done with him ?"

The reply was :

" Take him to the station-house and protect him.
                                                            " T. C. ACTON."

At twenty minutes past six the Twenty-eighth reported gloomily :

" Deputy Marshal Borst reports that the company of soldiers that he went with to Twenty-ninth Street has been repulsed."

And this was but one of several temporary re-verses now occurring at different points.   The rioters were much better armed now than they had been at the outset. They had even attempted obtaining artillery, as well as the organization of a cavalry force with the "Red Bird" omnibus horses. At half-past one o'clock, this day, this telegram of warning had been sent to the Sixteenth Precinct:

"Send a messenger to the Twentieth, in citizen's dress, to inform them they have a large force there with cannon."

The piece the mob had obtained was afterwards recaptured from them, as will be related. Without suitable ammunition and artillerists it was little better than a scarecrow, and was a heavy matter to drag around the streets. No harm whatever was accomplished by means of it.

At 6.35 o'clock word came from the Twentieth Precinct:

"Bombshell-factory, Twenty-fourth Street and Tenth Avenue, will be burned to-night. Carts have been placed across streets by mob. Also a number of other factories. A force should, if possible, be here in station to-night."

There was a look of revolution, of barricades and destructive ambition, about that, and it was duly attended to by the military as well as police. The blow at the bombshell-factory might indicate a vague idea that the mob was opposing all army supplies, but the threats against the other factories were more entirely in character. These were to be destroyed as property, and for no other reason, unless the working-men of the city should be on hand in time to prevent it.

President Acton had done all he could to save the doomed block of buildings at Second Avenue and Thirty-fourth Street. He had no men of his own to send, and telegraphed in vain to military commanders. They also were helpless at the moment, and no fault was to be found with them.

Complaints of weariness now began to come in from both police and soldiers "in the field," accompanied by urgent requests for relief with which it was almost impossible to comply. All had done their duty well, and had honestly earned their fatigue. It is to be recorded, as admirably illustrating the personal character of the Metropolitans, how frank and manly and generous was the testimony given by the police to the courage and efficiency of their soldier-comrades. There was no sign of petty jealousy. Men who are doing their own duty well can afford to praise the like good conduct in other men. At ten minutes past 7 o'clock P.M. the Sixteenth Precinct telegraphed:

"The military clear the mob wherever they go, and unless we keep them here the mob will burn our building down to-night."

At 7.38 P.M. the Twenty-sixth Precinct telegraphed:

"Ask Mr. Acton if the military shall take charge of a rifle-battery at *Times* office."

It was a curious question to raise, and he responded:

"If the military can do that, do it."

The rapidity with which changes occurred and were reported, and their multifarious nature, was enough to confuse the clearest mind, at times. The changes themselves arose from the conduct of those whose confused and disordered intellects may fairly be classed as insane for the time being.

At half-past eight o'clock Mr. Acton inquired of the Tenth Precinct:

"How are things?"

13

and was answered:

"Great excitement about burning different places in the precinct; and no men to keep them off, if so."

The Tenth had been more quiet than some others, all day, and its force had been employed elsewhere; but such attention as was possible was now given to its increasing necessities.

It was growing dark at last, and the second night of disorder and horror was settling down over the bewildered and all but panic-stricken city.

At twenty minutes past eight o'clock a despatch went out to all the precincts from the Central Office:

"Are there any troops in your precinct?"

and all but the Eighth responded, " No." That replied:

"None but disabled soldiers in this precinct."

At that hour, therefore, every station-house was a fort under the sole protection of the police, " specials," and citizens, the soldiery being out-side and operating independently.

The Metropolitans could indeed maintain their

own garrisons, but they were weary with hot and exciting work. Many who were still on duty had cuts and bruises to show. Many had been entirely disabled, and some had been killed. There was hard work yet before them, but a remarkably cheerful spirit prevailed, and no man expressed any doubt of the triumphant result.

At 8.40 o'clock a despatch from Mr. Acton to the Twenty-sixth Precinct said:

"Send a force immediately to the corner of Catherine and Cherry streets. Brooks's clothing-store is attacked."

There was trouble already in the Twenty-sixth, and the reply came:,

"The police of no use. The military we cannot spare them."

This did not mean that the Metropolitans were losing confidence in themselves, but that not enough of them were at that precinct, in good condition, to be of any use against such a crowd as was then known to be on Catherine Street. The rioters of that vicinity had determined that for once in their lives they would be fashionably dressed, and they had gathered an exceptionally large marauding party with a view to new outfits all around. An immediate effort was made to check · so grand a burglary with the nearest forces available. Help for the Twenty-sixth had already set out, and in ten minutes more, at 8.50 P.M., President Acton inquired of them:

"Have reinforcements reached you yet? If they are not enough, can give you more."

The reply was a fair commentary upon the habitual accuracy with which he timed and estimated the movements of his men, for it read simply, " Plenty."

The universal skirmishing was now lively in many quarters of the city, with fires occurring here and there to add to the tumult and confusion. At 9.35 o'clock the Fourth Precinct telegraphed:

"The crowd has attacked Brooks's store. One man shot. Corner of Catherine and Cherry streets."

The first attack, already mentioned, had been defeated by the rapid movement and sharp fighting of a force of police from the Fourth Precinct. It was not easy to obtain correct news from that vicinity, and at five minutes past ten o'clock the Fourth was asked:

" How are things now ?"

The answer came at once :

" Very bad.   I understand they drove the police at Brooks's.   Three of our men hurt."

Mr. Acton had been beforehand, as usual, and in ten minutes he was able to respond :

" There will be a force of military and police there in a few minutes."

The Fourth again replied :

" Send them to the corner of Oak and Catherine streets, at the gun-store."

Arms as well as clothing were included in the purposes of that mob, and Mr. Acton sent word :

" They have gone to Brooks's store.   Meet them and inform them of the location."

The store was well plundered before the rein-forcements arrived ; but they came at last, and there was a brief, hard struggle with them.   At 11.22 o'clock Mr. Acton again asked :

" How are matters now at Brooks's ?"

And the Fourth was able to tell him :

"We have possession. All correct."

Nevertheless, for some time after the suppression of the riots a part of the population of New York was distinguished by the newness, style, and very bad fit of at least a part of its wearing apparel. No time had been given the wholesale burglars to select and try on the goods.

At 10.35 o'clock Mr. Acton asked of the Fifth Precinct, on a suggestion brought by a messenger:

"Is there any trouble in York Street?"

The answer was grimly distinct:

"Yes. The mob is at work demolishing the whole row."

All over the city the cloud of gloom and terror seemed to be settling more and more heavily down. At a quarter before eleven o'clock the Twenty-ninth Precinct telegraphed:

"We want assistance immediately, as boys are setting fire to private dwellings and robbing them."

They were informed:

"A force will be sent you immediately."

But a precisely similar state of things was reported from other quarters. The " hoodlum" element was fast coming to the front, and the sons of rioters were following in the footsteps of their fathers.

The long struggle in the Eighteenth Precinct flared up again, and the rioters appeared there in strong force. The combined police and military were for a time unable to make any considerable headway against them, and at twenty minutes past eleven o'clock the Tenth Precinct reported:

" The Eighteenth Ward station-house is in flames."

The rioters had actually stormed and captured it at last, but the struggle went on in the midnight streets just the same, until they were scattered.

Sharp fighting had now for some time been in progress in the Fifth Precinct, and little was yet known of the result. At a quarter before twelve o'clock President Acton inquired of them:

" Is Inspector Carpenter in your precinct with his force ?"

The reply had in it solid comfort for him:

"I think not; but the military is, and is doing good execution."

Just how much execution they did, there and elsewhere in their several expeditions, that night, there is no record. Like the Metropolitans, they came and went as their services were demanded, and they were not firing blank cartridges any more.

Renewed attention had been given to the security of the gas-houses, but all the precautions taken were none too great. They were threatened again and again. As late as 10.25 o'clock the Thirteenth Precinct was directed:

"Send a man in citizen's clothes to gas-house foot of Fourteenth Street, and ascertain if there is any difficulty there.'

None was discovered, for the excellent reason that the gas-house was strongly garrisoned by U. S. regular infantry and armed citizens, who had turned it into a very respectable fort for the occasion, and were amply able to hold it. Still it was not a safe place for a man in uniform to go to or come out of.

In the course of the evening the two officers in charge of the Fifth Precinct station-house were advised of an approaching attempt at its destruction on especial account of some four hundred colored people who had taken refuge there. The colored men offered to fight for their own lives, and were supplied with arms. The doors were barricaded, and the brace of Metropolitans, Sergeant Higgins and Doorman Palliser, encouraged their black "specials" to hold the fort. The mob assembled and began firing upon the building at about ten o'clock. They were also attempting to set it on fire when Inspector Carpenter, with his somewhat ubiquitous and roving command, came upon them from the rear with a sudden rush, and scattered them in all directions.

The Inspector's evening campaign was a busy one, for at seven minutes past ten o'clock a telegram came to the Central Office from the Twenty-sixth Precinct:

"Ins. D. C. has met the mob that came down Broadway. Licked them and dispersed them handsomely."

The second day of the riot had now rounded to its close. It may be fitly characterized as a day of incessant skirmishing at a hundred different points. Many private houses had been broken into and robbed and some of them had been burned. A number of stores had been more or less thoroughly plundered, and the drinking-places had been made to do a large but uncommonly profitless trade. The weather had been hot, but so nearly breezeless that fires kindled had not spread unduly, and for most of these the firemen had worked very well. Even those of them who were opposed to the Draft had recovered their senses and perceived the separation between this mob and politics.

There was no pause in the fighting because of the lateness of the hour. At a quarter before midnight the Twentieth Precinct telegraphed:

"The mob has just driven the colored people out of houses in Thirty-sixth Street near Seventh Avenue. They fled here for shelter, but, as I was full, I sent them to the Sixteenth Precinct.'

It is not easy to deepen such a picture as is presented by that despatch. Murder had accompanied the turning out of the homes, and these had been burned to the ground with such of their contents as had not been carried away as prize. There had been no police nor military force unoccupied by other pressing duties, that it might be sent to prevent or to rescue. The nearest place of public refuge was full of similar fugitives, and no private householder dared insure the destruction of his own home by receiving them. A shuddering and frightened walk must theirs have been, men and women and children, through the midnight streets, knowing that the wolves of the mob were likely at any corner to pounce upon them. Sending them away from the station-house must have been a mournful sort of necessity to the officers in charge; but there was no help for it, and they reached their place of refuge in safety.

The last "general order" went out from the Central Office at 10.15 o'clock:

"Give the greatest care to your wounded men. ACTON."

It emphasizes the relations which existed between the men and their commanding officer. Hardly any other element of the police efficiency of that day was of greater value than their strong confidence in themselves and in the men chosen to lead them. The opposite of this would indicate decay and prophesy disaster. In every collision with the many bands of rioters, the inspector or captain or sergeant in command is described as having charged well in advance of his line. Men are apt to follow close upon the heels of that kind of leader.

The gas-works on the North River at Forty-second Street were of secondary importance, furnishing illuminating material to a limited area, and they had not been understood to be menaced. In the course of Tuesday evening, however, they were utterly destroyed, with the ferry-house at the foot of Forty-second Street, by a detachment of the mob too strong to be resisted by the small force in charge. There was no discernible connection between gas and the Draft, but deeds of darkness could best be done in darkness, and anything which suggested light or was used to produce it was an evident enemy of the riot. The other and more extensive gas-works had already been pretty well guarded, as has been related, but became objects of vastly-increased solicitude after this unmistakable warning.

Among the other old military organizations which held meetings of their own on Tuesday was the Ninth Regiment, N. Y. S. N. G. This was one of several militia regiments which, at the outbreak of the Rebellion, entered the national service almost entire. It did so as the " Eighty-third N. Y. S. Volunteers " of the "Two Years'

Service." It had now returned but recently, and rallied promptly under its commanding officer, Lieutenant-Colonel Rutherford. Many of its men came in at once on Tuesday, and enough more speedily followed to bring it up to a fairly effective standard as to numbers.

The condition of affairs in the city of Brooklyn, under Police Commissioner Bergen, was every way satisfactory at the close of Tuesday's operations. There had been much anxiety, but not many serious disturbances, and these almost altogether along the East River water-front. The necessary withdrawal of the Metropolitans seemed at first to leave the city almost unprotected, but President Acton comprehended the situation better than other men, and knew with what elements he was dealing. He had not been guilty of imprudence. The criminal classes of Brooklyn understood that their best opportunity for plunder was prepared for them in the streets of New York. Any robber or murderer or incendiary who knew his professional rights and proposed to enforce them was self-"drafted" to serve with his fellows on Manhattan Island as effectually as if they had previously enrolled him. That a few remained and accomplished a certain amount of mischief brings out only the more clearly the fact that the great majority were absent. For fear of these few remaining, however, the citizens of Brooklyn promptly bestirred themselves. They had a great advantage over their New York neighbors in being able to walk about through their own streets in safety. At the published call of the sheriff of Kings County they rapidly gathered, and armed in sufficient numbers to garrison the police stations and other important places, under the immediate command of Commissioner Bergen. To this efficient officer the credit for the comparative quiet maintained in that city from first to last is largely due.

The hours from midnight until sunrise passed gloomily enough for the people of the great metropolis. A large part of them did not so much as undress or go to bed, but sat up and listened to the strange medley of unaccustomed sounds which came in from the outer world — shouts, cries, screams, rattling musketry, the multitudinous rush of passing crowds, or the steadier tramp of marching columns of men. It was not considered safe to sit at open windows for fear of spitefully-hurled missiles or stray bullets, but stolen glances up and down the streets gave the watchers plain indications that the conflict between crime and the law was by no means over.

Large parts of the city below Fortieth Street were in almost undisturbed possession of the rioters. There was no patrolling done there by private watchmen or by police. Through street after street roamed gangs of ruffianly men and depraved, half-grown boys, breaking into dwellings, robbing, and perpetrating numberless acts of unrecorded villany. More and more was the great riot depicting its true character as an aimless outbreak of lawlessness, without one solitary redeeming feature exhibited at any time or place. It furnished a perpetual lesson as to the need of force, and plentiful force, and of its prompt and vigorous application for the suppression of every similar outbreak, whatever its apparent or asserted excuse. Only by the measures taken at an early hour for the protection of the main gashouses had the city been delivered from the horror of passing that dreadful night in utter darkness. Even the street-lamps and the lights in all the windows were a powerful reinforcement to the police and a restraint upon the rioters.

The more desperate of these indeed were them-selves compelled to rest a little, and the stupor of drunkenness had disabled not a few.

President Acton occupied himself during the remainder of the night in receiving all attainable information, and in arranging his plans of action and details of men for the morrow. His frame was tough and sinewy, and he had not as yet dis-covered in it any symptoms of fatigue. He had immediate demands upon him, nevertheless. At five minutes past twelve o'clock he telegraphed the Fifth Precinct:

" How are things now ?"

And obtained for answer:

" The mob was gathering fast to attack our [station] house, they having heard we had colored inmates, but the military came in time to scatter them. It is peace and quiet now."

It was the kind of peace and quiet obtained by the bayonet and the bullet; and at the same mo-ment Mr. Acton was compelled to telegraph the Twenty-ninth Precinct:

" Send out a messenger and find our men. We want them."

In ten minutes he was answered:

" The messenger says they are going down-town."

They were needed there, for already at ten minutes past twelve o'clock a telegram from the Thirteenth announced:

" Matters are worse in Grand Street."

Mr. Acton replied in about five minutes:

" How are things in Grand Street? Has the force arrived yet?"

And was answered:

" Lively. Store-keepers have fired into mob. No force yet."

At 12.20 o'clock A.M. he sent word to the Thirteenth Precinct :

" We will send force to Grand Street in a few minutes."

He had good cause for anxiety as to all that region, and in five minutes more he asked again, " How are things?" and was answered, " Very bad." The disturbance thereabouts did not go down at all, but it was still a " lively" neighborhood in the morning.

14

The Twenty-first Precinct was also having a hard night of it, and at 12.20 A.M. telegraphed:

" Building corner of Second Avenue and Thirty-third Street on fire.   Set on fire by the mob."

Direct communication was at that moment cut off for the time, and the next word from them came through the Fifteenth Precinct:

" Send assistance to the Twenty-first Precinct.   They are about attacking it."

Mr. Acton replied:

" Our force are on their way.   Will be there shortly."

At half-past twelve o'clock the Twentieth Precinct reported:

" The mob was in the act of demolishing the colored church in Thirtieth Street between Seventh and Eighth avenues, when our force rushed on them and they gave way—badly hurt."

This was somewhat indefinite; but the reasonable interpretation was that the hurt had been received mainly by the scattered rioters, and the meeting-house of the colored Christians was permitted to stand in spite of the rage of the heathen.

At ten minutes before one o'clock the Twenty-sixth Precinct reported:

" It is reported that the government store in Greenwich Street is on fire. Fired by the mob."

It was only too true, and was accompanied at the same moment by a despatch from the Thirteenth Precinct:

" The man has returned from the Eleventh Precinct. Reports a number of bands of robbers, numbering from fifty to one hundred. Breaking into stores in Houston Street near Attorney Street."

Messages were flying fast, now, by wire and by all other means available. At the same second of time one was delivered from the Twenty-ninth:

" I am told there is no officer in charge of the Twenty-first Precinct station-house. The mob cleared them all out."

This was true enough; but there had been few men there to be driven, for almost the entire force of that precinct was out in the sultry streets, battling with the rabble and protecting private dwellings from robbery.

Continual reports came in of "turning colored people out of their houses," but the brief despatches failed to more than suggest the countless cruelties which inevitably accompanied those merciless evictions.

So little was known by men who were fighting in near neighborhoods of the fate of their comrades, separated by a few blocks of buildings, that at eight minutes past twelve o'clock the Twenty-first Precinct asked of the Central Office:

"Have you heard recently from military sent to Eighteenth Precinct? Report here is that they have received rough treatment from the mob."

There had been rough treatment on both sides, but the answer was:

"They have returned here. All right there."

Which did not refer to the condition of the station-house for further use.

A remarkable example of the misuse of words occurred at a quarter-past twelve o'clock. A general inquiry was sent out to every precinct in the city of "How are things," etc., and without

one exception they responded, " All quiet."
Each operator knew he would be understood that
the war was progressing steadily, with no new or
suddenly exciting feature ; but the " quiet" was
that of Babel in a fever. The Eleventh Precinct
added :

" The citizens are rendering me much aid."

Ten minutes later the Twenty-first Precinct
also reported :

" One or two fire companies have rendered us good
service by driving the plundering mob away from their
work."

They were also doing good service by deepen-
ing the line of distinction between " the plundering mob" and respectable and self-respecting
working-men.

The mob still retained actual possession and
control of large areas, including long reaches of
the principal streets and avenues. Much territory
on the " East Side" was altogether their own.
At 12.35 Mr. Acton again asked of the Twenty-
ninth Precinct :

" How are things ?"

and received a more perfect definition of the word "quiet," for they responded :

"All quiet as far as we have heard from. Our scouts have not come in yet. That negro lies in Twenty-eighth Street yet. We have not force enough to get the body."

It was a strange announcement indeed, and offers a perfect mirror of the situation. A beleagured police force, worn out with its faithful performance of duty, sending out "scouts" to ascertain the whereabouts and operations of the public enemy, and frankly confessing that the field of battle and the bodies of the dead were as yet in the enemy's power. Mr. Acton himself could do no more at that juncture, and he replied:

"Towards morning send out and get that body when it will be more quiet."

It was four o'clock in the morning when he was informed that his order had been complied with. At that hour the Twenty-ninth reported:

"I sent the whole force to take the negro's body to Bellevue Hospital."

Any smaller squad might but have been compelled to prepare more bodies for removal, or else to have left some of their own to keep that black one company.

To the eyes of another man, the aspect of affairs was somewhat dark and unpromising; but President Acton felt that he was justified, at two o'clock that morning, in sending out words of encouragement to good citizens generally. The *World, Journal of Commerce, Tribune*, and other newspapers not specified in his order, were officially informed and were requested to announce: " The police have control of the city."

It was entirely easy to misinterpret and misrepresent that despatch, both at the time and afterwards, and the rioters themselves ridiculed it hilariously. Nevertheless it was only upon a superficial reading either over-sanguine or even premature. The sleepless Commissioner of Police knew many things which he could not explain in a despatch. He had made careful estimates of the forces under his command, and was aware of the strength of the other forces hourly coming to his aid. He knew that the mob had already called out its utmost resources, and that before long it must needs show signs of exhaustion.

The most quiet season yet experienced was from this hour until breakfast-time. Both sides were more or less busy with preparations for the hot day's work before them, and the leaders of the mob seem also to have considered that as yet they were having the best of the struggle. They could confidently have assured all editors: "The mob has control of the city, and is about to have more of it." They believed it, and from their side of the case they were not without reason. They had done a great deal of mischief, and had not been crushed out, and that of itself was a kind of victory. Their ignorance of the facts carried them right along, in blind, unreasoning presumption, and they succeeded in rallying their wretched followers in tremendous and unexpected force.

XI.

The Fighting on Wednesday.

WEDNESDAY, the 15th of July, 1863, was one of those sultry days of midsummer when any kind of bodily exertion is a burden. It was not a working-day for the majority of the people of the city of New York. They had little to do but to remain at home, anxiously awaiting the course of events. Except where tumult and strife reigned, or where smoking ruins attracted disorderly crowds, or within the areas where a remnant of business activity was protected by armed forces, the streets and avenues were generally vacant. With one exception, Sixth Avenue, the street-car and omnibus lines had ceased to run. The carts and drays were not carrying their accustomed burdens of merchandise, but were laid up where they could not be obtained for use in constructing barricades. Now and then a rapidly-driven carriage rattled over the pavement or a frightened foot-passenger hurried along the sidewalk, in token of some errand the importance of which justified the risk of life and limb. Those who took such risks did so under pressure of the awful knowledge that at any moment a pack of wolves might rush upon them. All things everywhere bore mournful testimony to the truth, so important to all men in this present time, that Anarchy is a deadly enemy of all the accustomed pulsations of human life.

At an early hour the slums of the lower wards began to pour forth thousands of marauders, savagely embittered against all authority by the resistance they had already encountered, and determined to surpass their own previous performances. They had still no defined cause or object on behalf of which to commit felonies, and the Draft had almost been forgotten by most of them. The wildest notions prevailed among them, and were freely uttered. One red-hot insanity declared was that they had in hand something like a social revolution. This was not at all their idea of a free country, which had proved to contain so many policemen and soldiers, and wherein " the people," as they gro-

tesquely called themselves, were forcibly re-
strained by armed and arbitrary power. Many
thousands of honest working-men were given a
sort of compulsory holiday by the closing of
their accustomed places of employment. So
were clerks and salesmen, for all the stores in
wide districts were closed. Such as opened in
the more quiet neighborhoods served their cus-
tomers at some risk of distributing their stocks
of goods gratuitously.

The five thousand liquor-shops within the
mob-infested boundaries kept open. Some that
closed their doors had them speedily opened by
thirsty visitors, and there was nowhere any dispute about change over their counters. It was a
time when the most tattered and penniless representative of "the people" called for such poison
as he craved, and was not refused. This was one
of the victories undeniably gained by the mob, as
it was about the last to be surrendered.

The morning papers of Wednesday published
such accounts of Tuesday's events as they had
been able to obtain. They also published
"proclamations" by Governor Seymour and by
Mayor Opdyke, and a number of military notifi-
cations and general orders. (See Appendix.)

ıe Brooklyn papers also printed importa
ficial notices.

Mayor Opdyke's proclamation had special rel
ce to persons holding for sale stocks of ar
d ammunition. He advised a cessation of sal
ıt the dealers in war-material had, as a ru
en among the first to close their stores. It w
vast importance to the results of the confl
at all ·the more extensive of these concei
:re within the business areas best and earlic
ıarded—such as Nassau Street, Maiden Lar
d John Street. Some less fortunately locat
d already been thoroughly plundered. Owir
ɔreover, to the stringent regulations governi
e storage of explosives within the city limi
e supplies of ammunition obtained by the m
fore or during the riots were by no means
ɔportion to their captures of muskets, rifl
:bines, shot-guns, and pistols. The miscellar
s character of their weapons rendered coi
ratively useless much of the ammunitic
:ually obtained, for it was in the form
·tridges made to fit special bores. They d
:ir best to make good their deficiencies, ar
t without a fair degree of success. The bra·
lonel Jardine, for instance, was severely woun

ed by a slug hammered down from a piece of leaden pipe. Other similar hurts were quite numerous, but the mob had no weapons to compare with the " dynamite bombs" of to-day's Anarchists.

In many respects, Wednesday was, to the Metropolitan Police, the most trying day of the riot. All of them were weary, and many of them were more or less injured. Some had succumbed to their exertions under intense heat, and others required all their pluck and sense of duty to keep their wearied bodies up to their work. They had been on duty night and day, with rapid marches and with much hand-to-hand fighting against strong and desperate men. Well might President Acton shout, as he did, with mingled humor and enthusiasm, from the front of the Central Office, to column after column of the men he was so proud of, as he hurried them off to their arduous and perilous errands :

"Go on, boys! Go on! Give it to them, now! Quail on toast for every man of you, as soon as the mob is put down. Quail on toast, boys!"

Late on Tuesday evening, as already related, several dwellings on Thirty-second Street, between Sixth and Seventh avenues, were sacked and burned. Their occupants were colored people, who fled for their lives to the nearest station-house; but some were not warned in time, and suffered various brutalities. One poor negro, lingering too long in his first hiding-place, was captured and dragged out by the rabble. He was horribly beaten, and then hanged to a tree. On Wednesday morning, at about nine o'clock, a force of U. S. Regular Artillery, under Captain Mott, was sent to clear the streets in that vicinity of the increasing mob around the scene of devastation, and to cut down and bring away the body. On their arrival the troops were at once set upon by the excited throng with more than common ferocity. After vainly giving full and repeated warning, Captain Mott fired with grape, killing twenty-five persons and wounding a large number. The mob dispersed, and the body was cut down, but an intensely bitter feeling was engendered. It does not appear that this was the first effective use of artillery, but it was the one most fully reported in the press, and it was commented upon with some severity by men who did not see the fight. Among the slain were found the bodies of several females (we can hardly call them women), as if to show that in every such aggregate of crime, here or elsewhere, the virago element is as desperate and dangerous as any other.

The number of arrests made had thus far been small. There had been no sufficient keeping-room for prisoners, if taken, nor men to be spared to guard them. In most of their collisions with the mob it had been quite enough for the police if they brought their own men out of the fray, not to speak of others. Nevertheless there had been here and there a well-clubbed rioter whose person had been almost unavoidably secured, and it was time to do something with these. At 5.45 o'clock A.M. of Wednesday, the 15th, the Twentieth Precinct sent word:

"We have ten persons arrested for rioting. Shall we send them to court this morning, or will it be dangerous?"

Mr. Acton asked:

"Have you men enough to take them to court?"

And on being answered, " Yes," responded:

"Send them to court first thing this A.M."

Before seven o'clock reports came in that the

citizens of the Thirteenth Precinct and others, outside of military commands, were arming them- selves, and that the volunteer and other military reinforcements of the police were increasing in all parts of the city. The people had manifestly recovered from the effects of their surprise, and were no longer in anything like a panicky state of mind. As to their first impressions, they had so long been accustomed to dwell in peace and security under the safeguards provided by the laws, that they had naturally required time in which to rally for so strange and terrible an emergency. The mob also was rallying for a desperate effort.

At 7 o'clock A.M. a message came from the Twenty-ninth Precinct :

"They are turning negroes out of their houses in Thir- ty-second Street. We have a lot of them just now here for protection. See what it is best to do, for I have no per- son here but myself and a doorman."

So early in the morning was all the available force of that precinct at work in the streets. The telegram was answered by,

"Is there much trouble?"

But at that moment the wires were interfered with, and all that the operator of the Twenty-ninth could transmit was the fact that he could not obtain anything from the Central Office. Communication was restored in about twenty minutes, and he added :

"Negro hanging on a tree in Thirty-second Street. By mob. Send us aid immediately."

The aid went, as described on page 222, in the shape of Captain Mott and his field-pieces.

Equally bad news began to come from other quarters. At half-past seven o'clock the Twentieth Precinct telegraphed :

"The mob are hanging negroes in this precinct, and the military are ordered down-town and have left. Send more forthwith."

Mr. Acton inquired prudently :

"What knowledge have you that the mob are hanging negroes? Or is it only rumor?"

The reply was positive :

"The officer that brought the order from General Brown for military to go down-town saw several. Others brought here news a few minutes before."

Mr. Acton responded:

" What force have you at your station ?"

and was told:

" Not a hundred policemen, and no military."

And to his further question,

" Do you want assistance ?"

came back an instantaneous " Yes."

Help was sent them at once, for a disturbance against which one hundred policemen appeared to be of no account manifestly required attention.

At a quarter before 8 o'clock A.M. the Fifteenth Precinct announced that no street-cars were running upon Sixth Avenue. For some reason the rioters on the west side of the city had not interfered with travel at so early an hour as had their brethren on the easterly avenues. It was done now, however, with but moderate loss to the car companies, for passengers were not likely to be numerous. All trade and traffic was under a sort of paralysis, and must needs wait until a cure could be effected.

The tokens of a tumultuous and exciting day

were increasing fast. Disturbances were reported from precinct after precinct. More and more frequent became interruptions of telegraphic communication. The bearing of messages was a duty by no means devoid of peril ; but orders flew hither and thither, and bodies of police and military fell into line and moved away in rapid succession.

Among other reports arriving was a further account of the sacking of the house of Mr. Sinclair, of the *Tribune*, on Twenty-ninth Street, the previous evening. The work was performed as a part of a vigorous search for Mr. Horace Greeley, and there was really something political in that, although his sins against the promoters of all sorts of crime and misdemeanor had been lifelong.

Another told of the destruction of a large dry-goods establishment in Avenue C by a rabble of about a thousand thieves. Over forty thousand dollars' worth of miscellaneous property was disposed of with extreme rapidity, and a similar process went on at other points all day long.

The U. S. Government had three large warehouses in the city, and to each of these a strong garrison was sent at an early hour.

At nine o'clock the Twenty-seventh Precinct telegraphed:

" The mob is going to sack the building on corner of Greenwich and Albany streets. A large force from Twenty-sixth Precinct is coming down."

It was not clearly stated whether the " large force" consisted of rioters or police, but the former had especial reasons for directing their operations towards the building indicated, as it was supposed to contain arms and ammunition.

So imperfect at best were the remaining means of intercommunication between the several precincts, that as late as 11.18 o'clock this very morning the Twenty-first Precinct inquired:

" Has the Eighteenth Precinct station-house been burned ?"

and was informed :

" There is nothing of it left."

Had the citizens armed themselves a little sooner a better report might have been made, for at 11.35 Mr. Acton was able to instruct his subordinates in the Sixteenth Precinct :

"Allow the citizens to take possession of the station-house and hold it "—

thereby setting its garrison of Metropolitans free to perform the more active service demanded of them in the streets.

The forenoon passed in uninterrupted skirmishing, the minor details of which are almost uninteresting from sameness. Among the sharper affairs was one in which a detachment of U. S. infantry commanded by Captain Franklin S. Reynolds was surrounded and assailed on First Avenue. The troops escaped destruction only by hard fighting and rapid firing. Between thirty and forty of the assailants were known* to have been killed and many wounded.

Mr. Acton's constant anxiety about the gas-houses led him to telegraph to the Eleventh Precinct:

"Look out for the gas-house in Fourteenth Street. Send some men there."

This particular establishment supplied gas to a large area included in the operations of the mob, and they had repeatedly made futile efforts for its destruction. Mr. Acton's attention to it again obtained for him the information that a sufficient force of riflemen had been sent to relieve those previously in charge, and the city lights were safe unless the mob should succeed in obtaining artillery.

At twenty-five minutes past twelve o'clock, noon, the Twenty-seventh Precinct sent word :

"I have just learned that there are twenty thousand muskets stored in the bonded warehouse 56 and 58 Greenwich Street, and the mob has threatened to seize them."

This, then, was the object of their   rning movement down-town. It was defeated, but if it had been made at an earlier hour of the riots it might easily have succeeded. It is worth while to consider for a moment how different would have been the history of the entire affair if the eruption had been directed by well-informed and intelligent leaders. Its main difficulty was that no intelligent and well-informed men had any part in its rising, whatever may have been the truth as to its original plot and instigation. The worst of criminals, with cultivated brains in his head, saw no temptation whatever before him, and kept away. It may not be so always. If the preliminary rush and surprises of July, 1863, had been aimed at such undefended repositories of arms as this warehouse, the Metropolitans and the first mere squads of marines and militia would have been hopelessly and helplessly swept out of existence. Twenty thousand muskets, with ammunition, or even with bayonets alone, in the hands of the rioters, and the returning regiments would have been called upon to retake a captured city instead of merely restoring order to one already in very good condition to be entered and occupied. Its retaking would be a matter of course in any case, but the destruction of life and property involved might assume the proportions of a national disaster.

The city Board of Aldermen came together at noon of Wednesday. With the speedy concurrence of the Board of Councilmen they adopted an ordinance appropriating $2,500,000 to pay the "exemption-money" of such drafted men as should be found unable to pay it for themselves. Methods for raising the money were duly provided. This was evidently done under the impression that the conscripted men were among the rioters, and would come out and be peaceable as soon as they were assured of exemption. It was a very great delusion, as the event proved. An appropriation twice as large would have been just as futile, for it would not have answered the real demands of a score of the real disturbers of the peace. The police and soldiery were attending to that.

The money appropriated was singularly close in its amount to the other total eventually paid by the city for the buildings which the mob burned down.

Some of the larger down-town printing establishments were still in operation. These were visited in the course of the day by deputations from the mob, with demands that all should be closed at once on peril of destruction. The deputations talked loudly and overbearingly. They had much to say concerning the increasing power and more perfect organization of the peculiar institution which they represented. According to them, it was about to take upon itself permanency, and supersede the worn-out concern known as "society," with its miserable edicts against theft and so forth. In almost every case their mandates as to "closing" were complied with, but it was well ascertained that they obtained no recruits from among the workmen.

The true nature of the outbreak was getting to be too well understood for that.

At quarter past three o'clock the Central Office was warned by the Twenty-ninth Precinct:

"The mob are firing the buildings in Second Avenue near Twenty-eighth Street. Assistance is required forthwith. The houses are occupied by negroes, and they are fleeing for their lives."

The men and women and children thus burned out of house and home and compelled to flee were native-born American citizens, with absolute and perfect right to live here unmolested. Their assailants were not so, and for the greater part were convicted offenders against the laws of the land. Yet there are many persons, at this very hour, in whose narrow and darkened souls all sympathy for the victims and all indignation at their oppressors nearly disappear upon information that the former were, as to their skins, " colored people," while the latter were only black in heart.

Ten minutes later the Twentieth Precinct reported:

"The mob are sacking houses at Twenty-seventh Street and Seventh Avenue. I have no force to send there."

Help went, but the aspect of affairs was now growing darker hourly, and sharp collisions with the fast-rallying rioters became more and more frequent. Collisions were also, as a rule, more bloody, from the more prompt and merciless use of fire-arms by the soldiery. But a small proportion of casualties were ever formally reported, and the coroner's office was almost out of date. In fact, four zealous coroners, earning heavy fees, had been busy day and night since Monday morning holding solemn inquests upon forty-three dead bodies. They had worked hard, and reported themselves tired out. More bodies were fast coming in now, and it became apparent that the perfunctory processes of ordinary administration of such matters had broken down. It was something like an attempt to hold an inquest upon the individual personal results of a pitched battle, skirmish-line and all.

The further assaults of the mob upon the telegraph-connections had rendered the wires entirely useless over large areas, and "breaks" were constantly occurring elsewhere. The police-telegraph repairers toiled devotedly, but could not keep up with the rioters, and messages were sent as best they might be.

At ten minutes before 4 o'clock P.M. Mr. Acton inquired of the Twenty-first Precinct :

" How do things look in your precinct?"

and was answered :

" Very bad.   The large crowd is in Thirty-fifth Street near Third Avenue.   Send us assistance from some ad joining precinct."

In about five minutes he again asked them :

"What is going on ? Give us the particulars."

And they told him :

" The mob has captured some five or six negroes, and is preparing to hang them.   Be quick with reinforcements."

It was a sad story to be told so late on the third day of the riots, but the best was done that could be done.   Help was sent, but it could not arrive in time to prevent the torture and death of some poor victims, whose only crime against even murderous ruffianism was that God had made them black and that their ancestors had been stolen into American slavery.

The requested report concerning the gas-house at the foot of Fourteenth Street came in at a little after four o'clock, and fully explained the fai'-ure of the rioters to provide convenient darkness for their next night's operations. It read:

" There are eighty-four regular soldiers in the gas-house."

Eighty-four trained riflemen, behind good brick walls, constituted an obstruction impassable by any mob which was now likely to be assembled.

The Sixteenth Precinct was able to announce, at fifteen minutes past five o'clock:

" Send us one hundred ' special' shields and clubs. The citizens are coming up well."

At 5.20 P.M. a seemingly dark piece of news arrived from the Twenty-ninth Precinct:

" The rioters are now at Seventh Avenue and Twenty-eighth Street. They have just killed a negro, and say they are going to cut off the Croton. They have pick-axes and crowbars, and also say they will cut off gas. So reported by one of our men, who has been in the crowd. They were about to fire the corner of Seventh Avenue and Twenty-eighth Street when he came away."

The demands for reinforcements elsewhere were

peculiarly pressing at that moment, and Mr. Acton was compelled to answer :

"You must do the best you can with the men you have."

The daring policeman who had risked his life as a "spy" no doubt obtained a correct idea of the will and intentions of the lunatics to whose ravings he had listened, but it needed only a moment of calm consideration to discern the narrow probable range of their proposed mischief. The Croton "mains" supplying the lower part of the city might indeed have been cut off, thereby causing much suffering and reducing the rioters themselves to whiskey as a sole beverage. The gas-pipes of certain districts could also have been severed, with much evil effect; but either operation would have involved a deal of steady digging, during which the diggers would have required much protection against interference by the police and military. No great or general damage could have been done save at certain special points, well known to the authorities, and along the main lines of the works indicated.

The Croton reservoirs were all north of the areas then under control of the rioters, and any expedition for their destruction would have required better leadership, as well as better following, than the mob possessed, and better tools than pickaxes and crowbars.

The High Bridge aqueduct, over which the great torrent of the Croton flows into the city, was six miles north of the operations threatening, and could be easily and promptly guarded. In these days of dynamite cartridges, the peril under similar circumstances would be something altogether different—that is, if a mob could be imagined again to rise with enough of stark madness in its fiendish folly to doom itself to die of thirst. Precisely such madness might be, with the help of rum, and the rage of continued repulses. In the present instance the action taken was prompt and very energetic. Much of it had been already prepared and was in swift progress, for it was only twenty-five minutes later, at a quarter before seven o'clock, that Mr. Acton telegraphed the Twenty-ninth Precinct:

" How about those pickaxes and the Croton ?"

And he received for answer:

" The military have driven the mob out of this precinct. I have not any further information. The mob has set fire to houses in Twenty-eighth Street between First and Second avenues."

Rifles and bayonets had temporarily settled the gas and water questions, but from the First Precinct had already arrived, at 5.25 P.M., this telegram:

" Riot at Pier 4, North River. They have killed negroes here."

The answer had been:

" We will send military help as soon as possible."

Just before six o'clock a despatch from the Twentieth Precinct said:

"Colonel O'Brien's body is reported to be in lot in Thirty-second Street near Second Avenue."

It was some other poor soldier's body; but whosoever it was, there was no force in that precinct strong enough to send for it at once, and none could be given.

At 6.40 P.M. a message from the First Precinct came in:

" Captain Wilson is here, and wishes you to inform Commissioner Acton that the residents are leaving Carmansville and Fort Washington [at the upper end of New York's narrow island]. They think the mob will be there to-night, and he would like to take his force up."

Mr. Acton responded:

"Tell him he can go."

He was the captain regularly in charge of that precinct, and at once returned for its protection. Such a raid as was suggested, into the thinly populated but wealthy districts away up on the western side of Manhattan Island, would have just suited the rioters. No soldiers were there, and but few policemen. The houses of the middle classes and the detached villas of the rich were alike unprotected, and contained much desirable plunder. There were also many negroes there to torture and to hang. It was a peculiarly helpless community. Had the mob obtained possession of the lower wards all imaginable raids northward would have been inevitable; but as it was they were now likely to have their hands otherwise filled, for their fate was coming in upon them.

XII.

Wednesday Night's Grapple.

THE third day of the great riots was now closing in upon the troubled metropolis, and only the police and the military commanders were at all aware how much had already been done, and how well, towards the ultimate restoration of peace and order. The citizens generally were contented not to venture far from home, even to obtain the news, although the hotels and other central and well-guarded places of resort were crowded at all hours with eager talkers and listeners.

So far as most men could discern, the aspect of affairs was to the last degree threatening, and all hungrily longed for the return of the absent militia regiments. Very few had any adequate idea of the extent to which the places of these had been gradually supplied by equally competent

16

veterans of the volunteer and militia and national troops of all sorts.

There were many Metropolitans to whose retaliatory minds the idea of rifle-practice upon their antagonists presented a continual and now constantly-increasing temptation. It was natural they should not like to leave all that work to the soldiery. They had been made targets of for mob-practice pretty freely, and hot days and nights of fighting and peril had by no means cooled their blood for them. At 6.40 o'clock P.M. of Wednesday the Eighth Precinct inquired:

"Will you allow us to have muskets if we find them ourselves?"

Every hour's experience had confirmed Mr. Acton's mind as to the wisdom of his original decision, that his men could do their best work with the weapons to which they were accustomed. He did not now propose to transmute good policemen into inferior soldiers, and he somewhat curtly answered:

"No.   ACTON."

Not even their many reverses seemed yet to have greatly diminished the ubiquitous activities of the rioters. Fires and robberies were going on everywhere. There was an immense amount of furious and aimless energy in the miscellaneous throngs who did all this mischief. What could they not have added, in all manner of destruction, had they but been a little better organized beforehand, and under any kind of central direction? Even as it was, there is a shudder connected with any imagination of what they would surely have done had they been less promptly met and less courageously and ably resisted, hour by hour.

The military forces were performing their duties most admirably, as the police continually reported of them to Mr. Acton ; but their detachments, like his own, were almost always confronted by superior numbers. The frequent occupation by the rioters of the dwellings or other buildings in the vicinity of any place of combat gave them decided advantages, rendering more difficult and perilous the operations of compact and disciplined bodies of men confined to the streets.

It was in turning the tables upon this kind of warfare that the Metropolitans rendered invaluable service as "skirmishers," whenever they could be on hand. They could do precisely what the soldiers could not. They could charge into houses and fight hand to hand, from room to room, and through the dark and narrow passages, while their comrades of the army or navy held their thin ranks firmly in the streets and avenues and stemmed the repeated rushes of the mob. Both kinds of warfare called for unflinching courage, and the dispiriting part of it all was, that no matter how well done a given piece of work might be, it was sure to require doing over and over. There were increasing indications that some of the more densely ignorant of the lower classes of recent immigration had got it into their dull brains that this was a "revolution" of some sort. By reason of this lunacy the rioters obtained many hundreds of courageous recruits.

The great iron-clad ram "Dunderberg" was in process of construction at Webb's ship-yard for the United States Government. A large force of workmen was employed upon her. These were real laboring men, of the kind this free country was made for and by whom it is governed. On Tuesday word was sent to the yard by the rioters, repeatedly, that the work must stop, and at the close of the day it was deemed best to suspend operations. On Wednesday only a small armed guard could be spared for the "Dunderberg," great as was the vessel's value; but the workmen engaged upon her had their wits about them. They mingled freely with the rioters, and discovered that their design was to capture and burn the ship-yard and the vessel at a given hour that night. The military commanders were at once informed, and a watchful scouting was kept up; but even then the threatened mischief was but narrowly escaped. During the day the members of the "old" Seventh Regiment, militia, with a number of the veteran members of the Twenty-second Militia Regiment, had gathered at the Seventh Regiment Armory. They were men to be depended on, and had rapidly been organized for service. A little before 9 o'clock P.M. about four hundred of these veterans, fully armed and equipped, commanded by Colonel Nevers, marched for Webb's ship-yard, to save the "Dunderberg." So closely had this movement been timed, that Colonel Nevers and his men actually caught up with the mob, about one thousand strong, on their way to the work of destruction. These were ready enough, probably, to assail any mere squad which might happen to be in their way, but were hardly prepared for a pitched battle with the serried ranks now bearing down upon them. There was a small "tussle,' but no firing. The bayonets were lowered for a charge, and the rioters broke and fled in all directions. The colonel and his men marched on into the ship-yard, and held it until morning without molesta-tion.

At a quarter before five o'clock the telegraph-wires to the Twentieth Precinct station and above were down again. Other wires were con-stantly interrupted. Only by constant efforts could a satisfactory communication be main-tained. The work required of the telegraph-wire menders is well illustrated by the first feat of Su-perintendent Crowley, already described. He did not seem to be aware that he had undertaken or performed anything remarkable. He rendered a great public service at the imminent peril of be-ing beaten to death, and that was all. He and his assistants had much more of that kind of per-ilous work to do in the course of the riots; but there is nothing picturesque or striking in the act of mending a broken wire. It is very common-place; not like leading a charge on a fine horse, with admirers and followers to shout and encour-age: but it is heroism, all the same.

From the very beginning of the disturbances a

peculiarly cruel and bitter-hearted fraction of the
mob had infested the western part of the city.
Scattered again and again, after their first exploit
of robbing and burning the Draft Office building
on Broadway, they seemed to reassemble as if by
magic. At about seven o'clock of Wednesday
morning one of their bloodthirsty gangs captured
and hanged a poor negro at the corner of Seventh
Avenue and Twenty-ninth Street. Another was
caught and hanged near the same place in the
middle of the day. But the crowning cowardice and fiendishness was perpetrated at about 7
o'clock P.M. The mob seized upon yet another
black man, and beat him in their usual manner.
They then hanged him to a tree, slicing his skin
with knives while they did so, torturing him to
death with the ingenuity of so many Apache red
men. When the poor fellow's body was afterwards recaptured and taken down by the police
it seemed as if hardly a square inch of his skin
was ungashed, and all his fingers and toes were
sliced off. It appears almost incredible, and a
deed not to be recorded; but it is only by the exact presentation of the doings of this mob that
its true character can be established. It must
not be left as a matter of any doubt, even at the

cost of reiteration, that the uprising of July, 1863, was not a "working-man's riot." Its true character must be set forth in plain colors in order that all men may understand what are the evil natures and horrible forces which are sure to be let loose by the temporary suspension of the laws. Even had the purpose and aim of the riot been in its outset a good one, which it was not, its breaking-forth would all the same have unchained these wolves from their dens of sloth and self-indulgence and crime.

The second negro slain on Twenty-seventh Street that morning was dragged out of his own house by his murderers, and was dreadfully beaten before hanging.

At about 6 P.M. of Wednesday, news came to the Seventh Regiment Armory that the mob was gathering in great strength on First Avenue between Eighteenth and Nineteenth streets, but it was not specified in the report how completely the buildings on either side of the avenue had been garrisoned and prepared. General Sandford ordered Colonel Cleveland Winslow to take a force with him and clear it out. He took about one hundred and fifty men of his newly-organized regiment, under Major Robinson, and a couple of howitzers, under especial charge of Colonel E. Jardine. The latter officer had distinguished himself before the beginning of these disturbances by the foresight, zeal, and efficiency of his services. The men he was commanding had served with him before on the fields of the Civil War, and he had a high reputation as an able and accomplished officer. Nearly all the force was ununiformed. The howitzers themselves, and two others like them, he had found and rescued from their hiding-places under a pile of rubbish at the Central Market, and he had managed to obtain suitable ammunition.

No sooner did the detachment make its appearance and undertake its appointed task than it was assailed by a dense mob in front, and by showers of missiles from the houses, including a brisk discharge of pistols and musketry. The fire from the mob in front instantly betrayed something like organization, for it was by volleys, given at the word of command. Here, at least, the rioters went into action under competent leadership, such as might have secured successes for them at many other points. Colonel Winslow and his men stood their ground courageously, and Colonel Jardine hurried his howitzers into position. He was none too soon with them to save the whole force from destruction. Ten rapid rounds of grape and canister tore through the masses of the mob and hurtled along the wide avenue. The slaughter was horrible, and the ground was momentarily cleared; but not so were the buildings on either side. The actual number of killed and wounded cannot be estimated with any accuracy, but there were rows of bodies on the pavement for about two " blocks." The fire from the houses grew hotter, and Colonel Winslow saw that he must retire. All he could do was to save his guns. Colonel Jardine fell by them, desperately wounded. A captain and a lieutenant of the Duryea Zouaves were killed. Every tenth man of the entire command was down, and others were falling fast, not to mention those who were disabled more or less by minor hurts. It was literally "decimated," and more than that, before it could escape. It was not possible to carry away the dead, or even the severely wounded. Of the latter, Colonel Jardine himself and two others were carried to a dwelling which opened its doors to them on Second Avenue near Nineteenth Street. Here they were daringly received and concealed, brave-

ly guarded and tenderly cared for, by some
patriotic ladies who risked their own lives unhesitatingly in this act of mercy. The story of their
heroism through the black hours of that night,
and while the infernal mob vainly searched the
house for the intended victims whose presence
there was more than suspected, lights up the
gloom with something brighter and higher than
romance. The noble-hearted women withstood
the most savage and bestial threats and verbal
insults, but did not for one moment betray their
trust. Others of the wounded were concealed
elsewhere, and it is not known that any living
man fell into the hands of the mob. If so, he
did not live many moments afterwards.

The military made good the retreat, and the
mob was left in triumphant possession of the
battle-ground. They held it until eleven o'clock
of the same evening. At that hour Captains
Putnam and Shelby, of the United States regular army, with one hundred and fifty men and
two field-pieces, well served, arrived to dispute it
with them. The troops were assailed in the
same manner as their predecessors had been, and
the artillery were at work immediately. A number of rounds of grape and canister were fired, at

close quarters, into the packed and furious throng, while the infantry poured in volley after volley, and replied vigorously to the fire from the windows. This latter was more a matter of intimidation than anything else, owing to the darkness; but the concealed marksmen labored under a corresponding disadvantage. They had had better light to shoot by in picking off Colonel Winslow's men. The regulars were not, therefore, subjected to anything like so severe a trial, while the storms of grape and canister swept the avenue until it remained in the undisputed possession of the servants of the law. Something like a victory was gained and punishment administered, but that was all. The troops held their ground until half-past twelve o'clock. Quiet seemed then to be restored, and they steadily marched away. As soon as they were gone, their scattered enemies again began to gather. It had been at no moment safe for the troops to break ranks, or to make an inspection of the effects of their firing. All they could report was that they had repeatedly opened gaps of a full block in length through the crowd, repeating the work of Colonel Jardine's howitzers. In both cases it was noted for future reference that about at the distance of two city blocks the fire of grape and canister is comparatively ineffectual, but that at short range no men living can hold a street before it. Had the Metropolitans been on hand to clear the houses, a more thorough result would surely have been attained.

While all this was going on, the contest raged hotly in other parts of the city. At about nine o'clock Mr. Acton telegraphed general inquiries as to the condition of affairs in all the precincts, and something like a temporary lull was reported.

The storm soon broke out again, however. Many fires were announced, occurring simultaneously in widely-separated localities. Had the Fire Department been in its best shape it would have been unequal to the perplexing task set before it. Well was it once more for the city of New York that there was no wind blowing to carry flames from house to house. A strong gale that night was all that was required to have reduced a large part of the metropolis to a heap of ashes.

At thirteen minutes past 9 o'clock P.M. the Sixteenth Precinct reported :

"Those batteries are in position. We exp
ack on the Arsenal soon."

That it could be expected at all star
great deal; but the fact that complete
:ions had been made for its reception
'or the other fact that the attack was n
The scouts of the mob may have been v
'ant fellows, but they could form some
in estimate of the discomforts of a bl
ipon batteries in position, well supported
nen.   The appearance of things near the
—or either of the arsenals or armor
strongly suggestive of war.   War it was,
war in which human society was fightin
very life.

At five minutes past ten o'clock the
Precinct reported:

"The negro quarters are in Sullivan Stree
iave surrounded and are going to burn it.   It i
iullivan to Thompson Street."

Help was sent, but much harm had be
iefore it arrived.

A telegram from the Twenty-ninth Pre
quarter before eleven o'clock, was nearl
f others of the previous night and this:

"We want assistance immediately. Boys are setting fire to private residences and robbing them."

Gangs of ruffians of all ages roamed hither and thither, seeking their places of operation as far as might be from probable interruption. They were giving the city invaluable "object-lessons" as to what might be expected of them and their kind at any time. The "control of the city" was in due process of recovery by the authorities, but it had not been possible, in the riotous districts, to do much for the restoration of order. There was no security of life or property save in the immediate vicinity of some kind of armed force, or in such dwellings as were held by armed and courageous occupants. There were many of these, as sundry gangs of marauders discovered to their cost. In the parts of the city above Forty-second Street a better state of things prevailed, and in some large areas lower down there was comparative quiet. The "away down-town" district of which Trinity Church marks the centre was one of these, as it had been from the beginning. Its vast importance had led to its being so well guarded and garrisoned that the mob apparently gave it up as an unprofitable undertaking.

A noticeable feature of many reports which came to the Central Office during this night was that so many attacks were made upon houses of ill-fame. In a majority of cases it was impossible to afford protection to the unhappy inmates. If help came to them at all, it came when sent for, and the sending could hardly be by any messenger from the house surrounded and captured. It was too late then. In several cases reported a good defence was made, and more than one brutal ruffian was shot dead upon such a threshold.

Messages from several precincts repeated the sad story, "We are overrun with negroes;" and to all was returned the same formula: "Give all people protection."

Midnight came and passed, and the turmoil seemed to subside a little. It did not cease by any means, nor could military or police relax for one hour their vigilant activities. The stout hearted men who were directing them went steadily on with their appointed task. This was Mr. Acton's third night of toil and care without one wink of sleep or one hour of rest. The preparations for the next day's work appeared to be going forward well. The Metropolitans were weary, but they were in good heart, and so were their soldier-comrades. These had already received important reinforcements, with news that others were near at hand. It was evident that whatever mischief was yet to be done by the mob must be performed within the next twenty-four hours, for after that the tables would be turned upon them.

.Precisely at midnight Mr. Acton's advices led him to send this despatch to the Eighth Precinct :

"The Seventh Regiment is reported to arrive at Grand Street soon. Send two men quietly to conduct them here to report to General Brown, and if they are not needed they will be dismissed."

He was a little out of the way, but not much ; for at forty minutes past four o'clock, in the gray of the morning, the Twenty-eighth Precinct telegraphed him the good news :

"The Seventh Regiment has arrived. Foot of Canal Street. They are on their way to Broadway."

It was the beginning of the end, to the minds of many thousands who speedily heard of their arrival. But the "Seventh" had not returned to be dismissed to their homes. They had hot and

17

perilous work before them. Their detachments were to do some street-fighting, and to aid materially in the restoration of law and order. If the seventeen regiments whose power they so well represented had been within call on Monday morning, there would not have been any riot to speak of,—and the city would not have been taught an invaluable lesson.

XIII.

Anarchy Dying Hard.

THE daily papers of Thursday morning were filled with fragmentary and very insufficient accounts of the various operations of the mob and its antagonists. A second proclamation by Governor Seymour, bearing date July 14th, although not published until the 16th, declared the existence of an armed insurrection. (See Appendix.) At the same time the Mayor printed another proclamation (Appendix), in which he congratulated the city that its troubles were diminishing and would surely soon be over. As a still further ground of hope, he made public a telegram previously received from the Secretary of War, but withheld as indicating to the mob a possible delay in the arrival of troops. It read :

"WASHINGTON, July 14, 1863.

"*To the Hon. George Opdyke, Mayor:*

" Five regiments are under orders to return to New York. The retreat of Lee now becomes a rout, with his army broken, and much heavier loss of killed and wounded than was supposed. This will relieve a large force for the restoration of order in New York.

(Signed)   "EDWIN M. STANTON, *Secretary of War.*"

The despatch contained other news of a cheering nature, although slightly incorrect in the view it gave of the fighting condition of General Lee's army. That held by General Meade at the time was probably more trustworthy.

The Governor, in his proclamation, had plainly set before the rioters the probability of coercive action by the power of the State. The authorities in Washington had been fairly deluged with letters and telegrams as to the progress and appearance of affairs in the city of New York. Senators and Congressmen and other eminent citizens urged their views of the trouble and its requirements upon the President and the Secretary of War, and there had been no small variety among the ideas thus presented. There had been some courage, much wrath, and many signs of panic. Numerous bits of information from Washington had been received in New York, and it was now freely reported, on the supposed authority of the Governor, that the Draft would be postponed, or suspended, or omitted, in com-

pliance with the demands of the mob. President
Lincoln was promptly questioned as to the truth
of the rumor. He replied, and his reply was at
once telegraphed to New York, that the Draft
would be enforced under all circumstances. It
had been interrupted by mob-violence, but there
had not been and would not be any wavering on
the part of the Administration in the performance of its duty. The President also refused to
put New York City under martial law until he
should be duly informed by the State authorities
that they were unable to cope with the existing
sedition. Until then, he said, he had no lawful
responsibility in the premises. All this was a
purely conversational utterance, duly reported ;
but it was as much as the occasion called for,
and Mr. Lincoln's thorough good sense was well
illustrated by the result.

It is not for a moment to be supposed, however, that Secretary Stanton so far neglected his
duty as to be in any manner dependent upon
chance medley reports for his understanding of
the riot. Every day a quiet-mannered gentleman
came on his behalf to spend some time with
President Acton and obtain the latest and most
comprehensive digest of the situation. The War

Office not only knew all that was going on, but at the end, when it was announced that all was over, Secretary Stanton telegraphed to Mr. Acton, asking him to name the man among the regular-army officers engaged who had best earned promotion; and the honor was instantly assigned to Captain Putnam, of the infantry. Notice of his advancement was at once sent to him, and he called upon Mr. Acton to express his gratitude. While he was seated by the President of Police, the officer on duty brought in a card and announced a gentleman by the name of Weed.

" Beg your pardon, Mr. Acton," exclaimed Captain Putnam. " Did I hear that name right?—Weed,—is it Thurlow Weed?"

" That is the man."

" Will you introduce me to him?"

" Certainly." And then came out one of the many romantic incidents of a great and busy life, for Captain Putnam owed thanks to Thurlow Weed also. After the battle of Bull Run, Mr. Weed was on the ground, doing all in his power and purse for wounded New York soldiers. He saw a stalwart volunteer half dragging a wounded comrade into a hospital tent, and followed to know if the injured man belonged to his errand. He did not; but the surgeon in charge attended to him rapidly, and then suddenly turned to his heroic young rescuer with,

"Here, my man. It's your turn next. You need attention more than he does."

He was bleeding profusely from a bullet-wound in the body, and was soon upon a pallet, commanded to keep still for his life, instead of carrying other wounded men. Mr. Weed was deeply interested, and remained at his side long enough to learn, with much difficulty, that the young hero had come to the front with the first detachment of Minnesota volunteers, but had lived in Ohio and Iowa. Then it came slowly out that he was born in New England, and was a descendant of old Israel Putnam of Revolutionary fame. Mr. Weed left him and went to Washington. He called upon Mr. Cameron, then Secretary of War, and enthusiastically but vainly pleaded for a regular-army appointment for the man whose unselfish courage had so won him. All the red tape then uncut was in the way, and Mr. Cameron could not grant the request; but Mr. Weed went at once to the White House. Mr. Lincoln heard the story, and with his own hand immediately wrote out

the order which made Mr. Putnam a second lieutenant.   In the following two years he had been
twice promoted, and was now a captain, just blos-
soming into a major for more heroism, but had
not seen or heard from Thurlow Weed since the
latter turned away from his pallet.

All this does not belong at all to the record of
the riot, and has no proper place in this book except as illustrating the wide difference between
the human elements brought into collision.   If
once a volcano is let loose, it costs the best kind
of blood to put it out.

The State did not call upon the Nation for any
help.   In fact, the State of New York, as such,
did not have any large share in restoring peace
to the metropolis, after giving all possible credit
to its very well-meaning Governor.   The Nation
did a great deal through its infantry, artillery,
marines, and sailors who were already on the
ground.   The services of these were invaluable.
Still it is fair to say that the city proved its ability
to rescue itself from its own savages.   The fact
was clearly demonstrated that its police, volunteers, militia, and other good citizens had the
necessary fighting strength to clear their own
streets of their convict and unconvicted invaders.

Secretary Stanton cheerfully telegraphed to Mayor Opdyke of regiments about to break camp and come home, and all such would be very welcome ; but other arrivals of outside help were much nearer than anything he could promise. There was enough of it to put a good foundation under the assurances of the Mayor and of the President of the Police Department.

At about ten o'clock of Wednesday evening, the Seventy-fourth Regiment, N. Y. S. N. G., arrived in excellent condition, and was at once placed by Governor Seymour under the command of General Wool. It was worth several proclamations, and Colonel Fox, commanding it, was ordered to report to General Harvey Brown for duty. That was practical co-operation with the police, and his work was at once given him. Before midnight of Wednesday, unexpected and unannounced, arrived the Sixty-fifth Regiment, N. Y. S. N. G., Colonel Brown commanding, and was similarly disposed of. It was a Buffalo regiment in fine fighting condition, and did good service in the streets on Thursday. The already existing organizations were increasing in numbers hourly, and here were two full regiments of capital soldiers to reinforce them.

The work of the day was well under hand, on both sides, by the time the citizens generally sat down to breakfast, such as they were able to obtain, and there had been some " activities" already.

The rural communities adjacent to the city on the north had been but little troubled by marauders, so busy were all these with their more important undertakings on Manhattan Island. On Wednesday morning, however, small gangs from the city, aided by a few local "roughs," destroyed the telegraph-offices at Melrose and at Williamsbridge, on the Harlem Railroad. From the beginning of their operations the mob seemed to be vaguely aware that all railways and telegraphs, all printing-presses, schools and churches, were on the other side of the fight.

Some of the city journals had not yet discovered the facts of the situation, and persisted in asserting a political name and character for the remaining marauders. Whatever of party politics opposed to the war and the conscription had been engaged in the outbreak had long since disappeared in the smoke of burning buildings, or had fled from hearing the shrieks of murdered men.

Before 7 o'clock A.M. of Thursday the reports which began to come in from the several precincts indicated another sharp day's work. At the same time the military commanders notified the Police Department of the increased and increasing assistance which they were now able to render. The pressure of the emergency had made itself felt in other places of power than those which employ secular weapons, and it was a time for all good and true men to do whatever they might be able. It was "summer vacation" for the Protestant clergy, and most of their churches were closed. Perhaps less responsibility rested upon them. The Roman Catholic Archbishop of New York was well known to be a good and patriotic citizen, highly respected by men of his own and of all other religious communions. He was by birth an Irishman, with a strongly-marked personality, and full to overflowing with the peculiar genius of his nation. He was old, and his infirm health confined him to his private residence. His knowledge of current events was such as his friends and counsellors might bring to him, and they evidently had not suggested to him earlier than Wednesday that he had a possible pastoral duty on his hands. Severe remarks had been made by journalists as to both the nationality and religion of the rioters, and these also had reached the eyes of the Archbishop. He at once wrote " An Appeal to the Irish Catholics from Archbishop Hughes," printed in the papers of Thursday morning, and a " Pastoral Letter," which appeared all over the city as a "poster," inviting his flock to gather at his residence next day and listen to him. (See Appendix.)

It was eminently right for him to do all in his power ; but if he had had a better opportunity for studying the matter he would have doubted his claim to many of the "sheep" then in the streets. None of the men who fought them suspected them of having any religion to speak of. The text of his utterances, printed and verbal, shows that he knew the nature of his own authority and understood his own people. He was not a civil magistrate nor a military commander, and he did not assume to speak with the voice of one. Still, by noon of Thursday all the supposable Catholics in the mob were aware that the head of their church in the city strongly condemned what they were doing, and it may have had some influence.

The telegraph lines to Boston were now all down, and remained so during the entire day :

but those to other points were less exposed and escaped the emissaries of the mob. The press reporters of the city labored under almost as severe disadvantages as before, but managed to gather column after column of miscellaneous information, with a general accuracy and moderation of statement highly creditable to their coolness and good sense.

From 7 to 8 o'clock A.M. notices were sent out to the several street-car companies to resume their customary running, and some of them actually made an attempt to comply; but their time had not yet fully come. At 8.35 a telegram from the Twenty-first Precinct informed President Acton:

"Officer Costello reports that a party of a hundred men stopped the Second Avenue cars on the corner of Twenty-third Street, and made them turn back."

That part of the city was still especially unsettled, for only ten minutes later the same precinct reported:

"Officer Johnson reports that at about 7 o'clock A.M. a party of fifty men chased a black man to Thirty-fourth Street ferry, beat him very badly, and then threw him into the dock and drowned him."

It was a peculiarly cowardly and sickening murder; but its record is a necessary part of the history of those dark days.

The aspect of affairs up to half-past ten o'clock, revealed by many inquiries, was such that it was decided to retain a strong military force at the gas-houses. The officers of the gas-companies published notices requesting strict economy in the use of gas, as so many of their employés were kept away from work by intimidation that production was seriously diminished. The Delamater Iron Works refused to resume without the presence of a sufficient force to protect their workmen. In all establishments employing many workmen a similar dread prevailed, for the mob had declared, from the outset, a bitterness of feeling in this direction which had little enough to do with the Draft Act. It came from a blind quarrel with capital which all working-men will do well to study with care, because its promoters asume to be their champions and to speak in their name as if they represented, or rather owned and controlled, them.

Scouting parties of police and soldiery were now sent out to patrol the city in many directions; and at first these brought in general reports of a

comparative quiet. Beyond a doubt, the fatigues
and excesses of three days and nights of rioting
had done their work upon large numbers of the
mob. So had the clubs and rifles and howitzers
of the defenders of the law; while the growing
strength of the military was an emphatic warning.

It was now possible to even begin searching in
sundry quarters with a view to the recovery of
stolen goods. The robbers had not been able to
provide concealment for such masses of plunder
as had been accumulated. Then and afterwards
considerable quantities were rescued from them.

At a little before noon Mr. Acton sent out a
general message to all the precincts:

"Receive colored people as long as you can. Refuse
nobody."

For they were still pouring towards the station-
houses, through any streets that seemed temporarily safe. When they could not do that, they
were hiding in cellars and garrets, hardly daring
to venture out for food.

Meantime the mob had gathered, here and
there, in sufficient force to resume active operations; and against these gatherings the efforts of
the police were especially aimed.

At 12.50 the Twenty-ninth Precinct tele-graphed:

"It is reported that the rioters are shooting down the military in Twenty-eighth Street near First Avenue."

There had been a severe skirmish in that vicinity which had not been reported to the Central Office at all, and is therefore an excellent example of many others, as important, of which even less was ever heard. At 1.25 o'clock P.M. the Twenty-first Precinct telegraphed somewhat more in detail:

"The mob has chased the military, about twenty-five in number, into Jackson's Foundry, at First Avenue and Twenty-eighth Street. The mob is armed, and every time a regular shows himself they fire. A few good skirmishers could pick off those riflemen and relieve the military."

Every effort was made, but it was forty minutes past two o'clock before the Twenty-first Precinct was able to announce, hopefully:

"The military has come."

It had been an affair curiously illustrative of street-fighting generally, and is also a sample of a large number of unordered, misdirected skirmishes.

This would have been unreported also, like the rest, but for its outcome.

At about eight o'clock in the morning a squadron of dismounted cavalry under their colonel attempted to disperse a mob on Third Avenue near Twenty - first Street. They were acting patriotically, but without effective discipline. They were at once fired upon from roofs and windows, and their position became exceedingly critical. A retreat began in some disorder; but the rioters pressed hard upon them, and they broke in all directions. They left behind them in the street the dead body of a sergeant; but most of the command got away, a part taking refuge in the foundry building. The colonel himself hastened to the Central Office with the news of his defeat, only to be severely reprimanded by General Brown.

"What are you doing here, sir?" demanded the angry veteran. "Go, sir. Your place is with your men."

Captain Putnam, with a full company of regular infantry and some Metropolitans, was at once sent by General Brown to the scene of the disaster, only to find it deserted by all parties. Attempting to continue their march up the avenue,

18

after recovering the body of the dead sergeant, they were suddenly pounced upon, as their predecessors had been, but with different results. The soldiers returned the fire, and the police charged into the assailing houses. After a sharp fight they felt justified in claiming a victory; but the place was a bad one to remain in, and they marched away, bearing with them a number of prisoners and reporting thirteen rioters killed and twenty-four wounded, so far as ascertainable, and how many more no one could tell. It was not at all the fault of Captain Putnam and his men that they did not then march on to the foundry; the soldiers there shut up were rescued at about 3 o'clock P.M.

The forenoon of Thursday passed, for New York City, in a continuous tumult, and a number of minor disturbances were also reported in Brooklyn. There, however, the condition of things reported by Commissioner Bergen was comparatively good. It was such that its mayor issued a congratulatory proclamation to the citizens. It was dated the 15th of July, and contained also certain strong recommendations as to further precautionary organizations of armed citizens for the maintenance of a more perfect patrol of the streets. This was evidently advis-able until such time as the Metropolitan Police could resume the performance of its accustomed functions. Over five hundred men were already under arms at the Forty-seventh Regiment Armory, and the German "Turner" societies had supplied an efficient patrol of over one thousand men.

By a little after 1 o'clock P.M. of Thursday the work of distributing the Sixty-ninth Regiment as garrisons of a number of important points was completed. It should be especially recorded that this excellent body of trained militia was composed almost exclusively of Irishmen. Had it been in the city on Monday, there is no manner of doubt but that it would have aided the many Roman Catholic Irish Metropolitans and their priesthood in redeeming that nationality from the disgrace and opprobrium cast upon it by those who hastily described the miscellaneous rabble as "an Irish Catholic mob." It was this which stung the worthy Archbishop. In no sense was there any "religion" mixed up with these riots. Nothing but aimless brutality and crime.

Having no religion of their own except, per-

haps, in name and in some sort of inbred super-
stition, the rioters very naturally struck blows at
any tangible evidences of religion in others, as
when they sacked the Five Points Mission
House.

The strength of the military forces now in the
city was such as to enable the overworked Metropolitans to obtain a little rest; but all who
were physically able remained on duty or quickly
returned to it.

At 2.37 P.M. this message was sent to the
Twentieth Precinct:

"Send some help to Twenty-seventh Street and Seventh
and Eighth avenues.   Trouble there."

The answer came at once :

" All our men are away, escorting colored people to the
Arsenal."

At 2.55 o'clock P.M. Mayor Opdyke telegraphed
to Mr. Acton :

" Has there been any disturbance since I saw you?"

and was answered :

" Yes.   Eighteenth and Twenty-first precincts.   The
military are there now."

The Mayor had proved himself a capable, courageous, and patriotic magistrate, and had vigorously co-operated with all other authorities and powers in constant consultation.

Other militia and some volunteer regiments were now arriving, or were announced as near at hand. The aspect of affairs had undergone a change which all men understood must be permanent, but the rioters were by no means disposed to give the matter up. Neither were the citizens ready to believe in their deliverance. There was a wide-spread feeling of dread, and of distrust as to further developments. The fear of the mob was so strong that it broke out, here and there, in curious expressions of pusillanimity. For instance, while the officers of the Twenty-first Precinct were engaged in providing quarters for the Seventh Regiment for the coming night, they were compelled to telegraph to the Central Office, at 5.25 o'clock P.M. :

"There is a room near Fourth Avenue in Thirty-second Street. Holds about five hundred. Balance we can accommodate. We found other buildings, but owners are out of town, and the agents will not take the responsibility."

The reply was instantaneous:

" Commissioner Acton says you will take the room and he will take the responsibility."

That was a "war measure" fully justified by the law and the facts; but the men must have been in a panicky frame of mind who deemed a building in danger of mob-violence by reason of having five hundred riflemen quartered in it, or who questioned the ability of the city of New York to pay for any and all damages.

At the same hour, 5.25 P.M., the First Precinct reported :

" The Twenty-sixth Michigan Volunteer Regiment has arrived and has landed."

Even the West was to have a hand in finishing up the mob in New York. Gross and dark must have been the stupidity and ignorance which had taken no account or thought of the power which could so quickly be brought to bear, for its destruction.

At 5.35 the following significant telegram arrived by way of the Twentieth Precinct:

" *To General Brown :*

"I have just taken a piece of artillery intended for the

use of the rebels. It lies corner of Fifty-second Street
and North River. What disposition shall I make of it?

"CAPTAIN SHELLEY, U. S. A."

The captured gun had required a company of
infantry and a sharp fight for its winning, and
there was a touch of soldierly humor in the veteran general's response :

" Use it against the enemy."

The despatches and reports of all kinds from
many of the military officers persisted in describ-
ing the rioters as "rebels," the soldier-mind
being apparently unable to regard them as any
other than allies of the Confederate forces in the
field. It was an instinctive perception of some
of the inner verities of the situation; although
few suppose that the Confederates had any practical agency in the riot.

The several detachments of sailors and marines
on duty in the city had now been organized under one responsible chief. They numbered about
seven hundred, under command of Lieutenant-
Commander R. W. Meade, U. S. N., as "the
naval battalion."

There had not been wanting, from the outset,
political notorieties of the baser sort who were

willing to take the part of the rioters in the hope
of future support to their personal ambitions.
That sort of thing is to be expected under any
circumstances. There were also newspapers, then
as now, capable of advocating almost anything,
but it is not worth while to record their utterances. A few selections from the nearest news-
stand to-day would serve a much better purpose.

The politicians referred to swarmed around the
Governor when he came, but did not succeed in
preventing his proclamations. None of them
called a second time to see President Acton or
General Brown about the matter, for reasons
given them in very vigorous English.

From about 8 o'clock P.M. until nearly midnight, detachments of various regiments marched
through all the streets, to and fro, from Fourteenth Street to Twenty-eighth Street, between
Second Avenue and the East River. They found,
of course, no enemy gathered in sufficient force
to oppose them, and that dangerous locality was
reported "quiet" for the first time since the
outbreak.

Late in the afternoon there had been a severe
engagement on Seventh Avenue near Thirty-
second Street, the particulars of which were

almost unobtainable, and which received severe criticism from the political friends of the rioters. The facts seem to have been that a mob there proved too much for a small police force first, and even a squadron of cavalry charged them in vain, and a detachment of infantry failed to clear the street. Artillery was not used until the last extremity, but was on hand and ready for action speedily. Two companies of the Eighth Artillery Regiment, under command of Captain John H. Howell, with a field-battery, opened at short range with grape and canister. Half a dozen rounds were rapidly fired, and the mob was thoroughly scattered. Of course the consequences were ghastly enough, and some who suffered were mere spectators. There may have been extreme severity, but it must be considered that this was the fourth day of the riots, and every man within range was fully aware of the responsibility he took in being there. At all events, the avenue was effectually cleared, and the disturbances did not again assume formidable proportions in that vicinity.

Precisely at midnight the One Hundred and Fifty-second Regiment, New York Volunteers, reached the city, and reported for duty to General Brown. They were at once quartered in the colored Methodist Episcopal church building opposite the Police Headquarters. They were a new regiment of " three years' volunteers," mainly enlisted in Herkimer and Otsego counties, and appeared quite willing to have a brush by the way with the kind of rebels that had risen in New York.

At the same hour, twelve o'clock, a message came from the Ninth Precinct:

"Our men are fighting the mob corner Fourteenth Street and Sixth Avenue."
"Do you want assistance ?"

inquired Mr. Acton; and when he received an instantaneous "Yes," he added:

"Do you want assistance besides the police ?"

And they answered :

"Not immediately."

Something of jealous pride spoke in that reply. The Metropolitans were decidedly unwilling to accept aid unless it was absolutely needed. They preferred to do their own fighting, unless really in danger of being overpowered. The struggle on Sixth Avenue was a hard one, however, and three quarters of an hour later Mr. Acton was compelled to send additional reinforcements. He telegraphed the Fifteenth Precinct:

"Send your reserve to the corner of Fourteenth Street and Sixth Avenue. They are fighting there."

The fray had then continued for more than an hour, and the mob had thus far manifestly held their own. Whether the soldiery took any part in it, or how it terminated, cannot now be ascertained. It was one of many similar affairs of which there is but a brief mention or a hint, to be found only in the telegraphic questions and answers and orders preserved in the Police records.

Between midnight and sunrise it may be said that the great riot died out; but it perished at any point only under pressure of overwhelming power vigorously exercised.

XIV.

Restoration of Order.

THE city of New York was in anything but a peaceful condition on the morning of Friday, July 16th. The mob understood that it was beaten, and yielded sullenly to superior force ; but its turbulent spirit was still manifested at every opportunity.

During the previous night the now numerous and comparatively fresh military forces had relieved the worn-out police of the perilous duty of clearing the streets. The Metropolitans had thoroughly attended to all that was left upon their hands, but in several precincts they had not even " scouted " to ascertain what was doing by the several detachments of soldiers who were marching hither and thither. Small blame to them if they were willing to rest, now that they could do so with safety. So little did they know of the details of the night's operations, beyond their own work, that at five o'clock in the morning the Twenty-first Precinct reported :

" I have just learned that there was a good deal of firing in the Seventeenth and Eighteenth precincts during the night. There was also considerable firing done in this precinct. There was one man shot dead in No. 150 East Thirty-second Street, he having fired a pistol at one of the soldiers."

There was no report made of the effect of any other than that one bullet out of all the many that were fired in those three large and densely-peopled precincts. Precisely the condition of the main thoroughfares is presented in a condensed form by the following question and reply. At 5.35 o'clock A.M. the Third Precinct telegraphed the Central Office :

" Do you think it safe for four colored women with children to go up-town to Sixty-first Street to their homes ?"

And the only answer that could be sent was, " No."

An interesting part of the morning's telegrams and messages to and from the Central Office were such as related to the quarters and provi-

sions of the military. There had been some un-
avoidable imperfections in the suddenly-made
arrangements for housing and feeding so many,
and there had been a little grumbling in conse-
quence; but the general success of the police as
quartermasters and commissaries is fairly represented by this telegram, which came through the
Twentieth Precinct:

" *To Mr. Acton:*
    " My men have received the best possible care and at-
tention from [Police] Captain Blott. We are on the alert
for the rebels."

Preparations were now making for a general
effort at the arrest of known rioters, especially of
leading spirits among them; but it was not yet
safe for messengers, on that or any other errand,
to go and come in uniform. It was needful that
any policeman passing through the streets alone
should be in citizen's dress, lest he should fall
into the hands of some yet undispersed band of
the vindictive and still dangerous mob. The very
punishment inflicted upon them had stung to fury
such natures as their conduct had already exhibited, and they were eager for every chance at re-
taliation.

There was even less depth of resentment, for some inscrutable reason, against the soldiery, although these were roundly accused of exercising too much severity, and of making too free a use of powder and lead.

On the morning of Friday General Harvey Brown was relieved by General E. R. S. Canby. A general order issued by the former (see Appen_dix) bestows a noteworthy commendation upon the Metropolitans, as well as upon the soldiers under his own especial command.

Mayor Opdyke published a proclamation (see Appendix) of an encouraging nature. He advised all good citizens of the impolicy of gathering in crowds of any sort, and urged upon them the duty of defending their houses, at all hazards, against the attacks of any robbers whatsoever.

It has not been possible to obtain an accurate list of the many fragmentary military organizations which from hour to hour fell into line and took an active part in the protection of property and in the suppression of the riot. Several of them were absorbed by the "minute-men" under Colonel Cleveland Winslow. Others attached themselves to larger bodies or were distributed among them. A list of such as were entitled to rank as

" regiments," without mention of mere fragments, will be found in the Appendix to this book, with quite possible omissions. All told, however, the force on Friday morning did not amount to more than two thirds of the strength of the seventeen militia regiments of New York and Brooklyn sent to Pennsylvania to reinforce General Meade's army. Had these been in the city there would have been no Draft-riot. Were an outbreak to occur to-day, the officers of the National Guard may be the best judges of its present condition as compared to its war-time strength in 1863. Outside of it, the veteran "volunteers" who rallied then, full of zeal and ready for action, have passed away, and no such effective force could be rallied now.

The returning militia had found duties awaiting them. One company of the Seventh, under Captain Emmons Clark, had a spirited skirmish with the rioters on Thursday. Others, in detachments from many commands, learned that the business of "stamping out" a mob meant almost that literal process. Besides various local fights, they were marched through nearly every street and avenue below Forty-second Street, with salutary effect. Men who could not or would not read printed proclamations could comprehend at a glance the meaning of those glittering rows of steel points.

Proper orders were given by the commanding general and the Police Department that there should be no interference with the Friday gathering at the house of Archbishop Hughes. At the appointed hour an immense throng assembled on the corner of Madison Avenue and Thirty-sixth Street, and the Archbishop kept his promise to them. He addressed them from his chair on the balcony, and his voice was strong enough to make himself generally heard. He spoke long and often eloquently, with many humorous or earnest appeals to national feeling and religious pride. His address was full of good counsel and of a sort of fatherly indignation which did not hesitate to employ plain language. He said, among other things:

" Every man has a right to defend his house or his shanty at the risk of life. The cause, however, must be just. It must not be aggressive or offensive. Do you want my advice? Well, I have been hurt by the report that you were rioters. You cannot imagine that I could hear these things without being grievously pained. Is there not some way by which you

19

can stop these proceedings and support the laws, none of which have been enacted against you as Irishmen and Catholics? [Cries of "Stop the Draft."] You have suffered already. No government can save itself unless it protects its citizens. Military force will be let loose on you. The innocent will be shot down, and the guilty will be likely to escape. Would it not be better to retire quietly?"

He urged them not to stain the name of Irishman and Catholic with deeds of cowardice and cruelty. His appeals were frequently interrupted by cheers, and sometimes by half-angry remarks or questions. There could be no doubt that he was addressing that part of the mob which really believed itself to be doing something in opposition to the Draft. The other and larger and more dangerous part of the mob which had been doing mischief for its own sake did not gather to hear the Archbishop. The multitude who had received his excellent advice dispersed as they came, unmolested by the representatives of the law; and before sunset not only they but every other considerable fragment of the tumult had decided that the time to subside had fully come.

It is not to be supposed that the city instantly resumed the ordinary machine-like operations of its municipal administration. There were minor disturbances here and there on Friday, and there could be no perfect patrolling done throughout the following night in all the dark corners of the city. The riot was over, however, and all men felt secure in proceeding to their accustomed avocations.

On Saturday, July 18th, General John E. Wool was relieved of the command of "the Department of the East," and the appointment of General John A. Dix made to succeed him.

President Lincoln made a peculiarly judicious selection of the right man for the place and time. General Dix was himself a New-Yorker, and had been governor of the State as well as United States senator. He had been a life-long member of the party politically opposed to Mr. Lincoln's election, and could not be accused of partisan feeling in any action he might take in support of the authorities. At the same time he added to the fruits of his wide and varied experience an uncommon degree of the "judicial temperament," admirably qualifying him for the responsibilities he now assumed. His published orders on taking command were marked by a dry brevity which was unmistakably clear. There was not a trace of " the politician" in them.

The militia regiments were now returning rapidly, and other forces were on their way to strengthen the garrison of the city and har-bor.

General Dix and General Canby were to have power in their hands which their predecessors had not, and all the seditious elements were aware of it. Moreover, the reaction of popular feeling caused by the excesses of the riot worked strongly in favor of the National Government and almost made the Conscription Act popular. Quiet people all over the country were ready to say, " Anything rather than anarchy."

The sums paid out of the city treasury after-wards, in compensation for losses caused by the riot, such as buildings burned down and their contents, are estimated at about two millions of dollars. This was but a small part of the actual loss, and the payment of it by the city did but distribute it among the taxpayers. The losses of business, of wages, and of many other kinds, were already assessed, and distributed themselves among the entire population. These were enormous. There was no working-man who did not have to pay a much larger share of it, in proportion to his means, than any capitalist. And so it must always be.

The loss of life by the mob is very difficult to estimate, even approximately. The police estimate ranges from twelve to fifteen hundred rioters killed. Well-informed military authority gives it at about thirteen hundred. A despatch to the War Office at the time, from an official in the detective service, reported the number somewhat too exactly at fourteen hundred and sixty-two. Of the wounded it needs only to be said that the death-rate in certain parts of the city was largely increased during the months following, and that the increase was not unjustly ascribed to this source by the health officers of the city.

The records of the month of July, 1863, show a notable excess in deaths and burials. For the "riot week" and the week following, two hundred and seventeen deaths from sunstroke are reported. During the days of the chaos, however, the Burial Permit Bureau was unable to attend to its regular routine of business for obvious reasons. It is not to be supposed that the corpses of slain rioters were kept above ground in hot weather until the accustomed formalities could be complied with.

On the part of the police and military the mortuary records are almost equally scanty. There were many killed and wounded, and no more can be said.

The churches of the city were not generally well filled on Sunday, July 18th, but those of the Roman Catholic faith offered a marked exception. They were crowded. The priests had a good opportunity to do their duty, and they did it manfully. Their denunciations of the rioters and their deeds left absolutely nothing to be asked for. They knew exactly what they were talking about, for they alone had been safe to come and go through the dangerous parts of the city during the entire week.

They were in no confusion of mind as to the true nature of all that they had seen and heard, and they plainly pronounced all the deprivations, penalties, and anathemas of the Church against the men who had been, or ever again should be, guilty of the crimes they had witnessed and now eloquently depicted.

With subsequent judicial proceedings this rec-

ord has very little to do. There were trials of
offenders, convictions, punishments. Something
was done, but not much, and there hardly ever
can be. The mob is not much afraid of the
courts. Anarchy does not shiver at the prospect
of being indicted; although the action of the
Chicago courts, concerning the anarchists convicted of murder there, looks as if the lovers of
American liberty were waking up to the perils of
lawless license.

The city was quiet, but there was a universal
feeling that its peace and civilization had found
its weak spot.

XV.

The Opportunity.

A NARCHY and the related forms of prepared crime watch by day and night for an excuse and an opportunity. Any excuse will answer, and any state of high fever will provide a sufficient opportunity. Such as came in 1863 might be paralleled or exceeded by entirely unforeseen occurrences at the present hour. The excuse and fever then arrived hand in hand, day after day and week after week. If the riot element in New York was at all stirred beforehand by secret agents of the Confederacy, as was then asserted, all such were of no importance whatever in comparison with agencies of another nature which are working now.

There is at least an historical interest in the exact state of affairs just before that 13th of July. A little more than two years intervened between the battles of Bull Run and Gettysburg. The trials, privations, and sacrifices of those two years had not fallen very heavily upon the New York mob. Such of them as worked had better wages than ever before.

For the nation as a whole the Civil War reached its darkest military day and its point of greatest unpopularity in the spring of the year 1863. Every description of discontent and of disaffection towards the Lincoln Administration controlling the National Government was at its climax in the early summer of that year. At no time before or afterwards was Mr. Lincoln himself so grossly underrated or so outrageously libelled by all his critics, patriotic or the reverse. And yet the struggle for the preservation of the United States as one nation was avowedly and unmistakably a war in the interests of free labor. It was distinctively a working-man's war, and was so regarded by most intelligent men in Europe and America. The starving Manchester cotton-spinners sent words of encouragement to President Lincoln, and the working-men of the Free States poured into the army, without distinction of race or religion or political party.

The drain of men for the army was not at any time in excess of the regular increase of the pop-

ulation, but it grew in steady proportions as the
area of the conflict widened, and armies of occupation were required as well as armies of invasion
and conquest. Under the volunteering system
the demand for soldiers was made to levy its
blood-tax altogether upon the patriotic, the unselfish, and the willing of all political parties.
There were enough of these for a season, but as
the days went by and the aspect of affairs seemed
to grow darker and more unpromising, the supply
threatened to become inadequate. As early as
the autumn of 1862 the gravest apprehensions
were justly entertained by the War Department
and the President. There were many causes at
work to diminish recruiting. There was less
enthusiasm with reference to military matters
as these became better and better understood.
The returning veterans of disbanded regiments
whose terms of service had expired brought home
with them no rose-colored pictures of camp-life.
At the same time such men justly considered
and declared that their places in the ranks should
be taken by others who had as yet borne no part
of the public burden. Even the liberal bounties
everywhere offered by States, municipalities, and
individuals failed to provide a sufficient stimulus.

There were more able-bodied men of military age in the country than when the war broke out, and a great many volunteers did come forward, but not in sufficient numbers.

On the other hand, a rigid system of conscription was in force at the South, enabling the Confederacy to call out its last available human being. In this state of affairs President Lincoln recommended an enrolment and conscription, and Congress, after careful deliberation, matured and passed a well-guarded law, commonly known as "the Draft Act," approved March 3, 1863. Under the provisions of this act the War Department was prepared to make a draft of men for the army from the entire population of the country in little more than four months from the passage of the act.

That such an iron-handed reaching out after the military services of the unwilling should be unpopular with them was a matter of course, but it was not and could not be unpopular with anybody else. It came upon the country, nevertheless, at the precise hour of the struggle when it was likely to excite the deepest and most determined opposition.

The really magnificent management of the

Lincoln Administration under its colossal difficulties was hardly understood at all; and its grand
military and naval successes were so habitually
belittled, that the war was looked upon by many
as but one long record of disaster and defeat, the
outcome of incompetence or treachery. Not even
the unanswerable figures of the successive election returns were sufficient to convince the popular mind that the number of voters in the Free
States had increased rather than diminished.

The people were heaping up riches faster than
they ever had done before, but large classes met
the demands of the growing burden of taxation
with delusive assertions of national impoverish-
ment and failing resources.

Another feature of the situation came fright-
fully to the front during the riots. Old political
partisanships and race antagonisms had been
aroused and stimulated to new and virulent
activity during the autumn and winter of the
year 1862 by the more pronounced anti-slavery
attitude of the Lincoln Administration. All
that remained of anti-negro prejudice was pro-
voked to a hitherto unknown intensity by the
Emancipation Proclamation. The war itself
could now be denounced as an " Abolition war,"

and the opponents of the Draft considered that they had made a keen thrust when they pro-tested against dragging free white men from their homes and families that they might be butchered for the benefit of the "nigger." Of the strength of this feeling among some of the lower classes of our imported ignorance little account was taken. It was not supposed to have any other means of expressing itself than in the press or at the polls. It was very much like some other surging bitternesses of which no ac-count is taken, nowadays.

The Conscription Act had been framed with studious care, that it might present as few fea-tures as possible of unevenness of pressure, or of other injustice or hardship. Among its thought-ful safeguards was the clause providing for ex-emption of a drafted man on payment of three hundred dollars or furnishing a substitute. (See Appendix.)

This furnished a rare text for anti-property as well as anti-war declamation; but all the unpatri-otic who could raise three hundred dollars, and all the men half-way willing to go, were contented to take their chances and abide by the result. The outcry against the "rich man's exemption," as it was called, was very loud, but there was not enough of it to indicate extended results of any kind. Those who said it would die out as soon as the Draft was over were entirely correct, as the result proved. There was just enough of a fever, as there is now about some other questions, to prepare for the " Black Joke" rush and a local eruption.

The National Government had a plain duty before it, and the War Department began preparations for making efficient use of the comprehensive power thus placed in its hands. General James B. Fry, a most capable and patriotic officer, was appointed Provost-Marshal-General.

The census statistics were appealed to for data as to the local distribution of population ; and the several reports of States and Territories as to numbers of volunteers already furnished were diligently compared with the census statistics, that due credits might be justly given in the apportionments of all quotas demanded. The entire loyal areas were divided into districts, all boundaries thereof corresponding with those of the existing Congressional districts. These in turn were mapped out into sub-districts, and each of these was provided with a local provost-marshal and his assistants. A searching enrolment was then begun, and carried to completion, of all men of military age; and the system pursued was so well devised and digested as to preclude so far as possible all favoritism or injustice.

This enormous mass of preliminary work required time for its elaboration and performance, and the enemies of the Draft were given ample opportunity for such opposition as was yet within their reach, and for brewing such further mischief as they might be able to devise. Of course there were able lawyers who were ready to declare the unconstitutionality of the Conscription Act. Of course all political leaders opposed to the Lincoln Administration denounced its heartless tyranny: they had carried the previous elections largely, and expected to make a clean sweep next time, as was their right, if they could. The very strength of that expectation bound them to the ballot, and forbade an appeal to the bullet or any other form of violence.

Whatever delay there was in the final enforcement of the Draft in the city of New York was due solely to matters of detail, and not to any vacillation on the part of President Lincoln, induced by the appeals of Governor Seymour. At

the same time the current official communications of the local deputy provost-marshals with
their chief at the War Department in Washington were not made public, and so an incidental
veil covered the precise state of advancement
of the final preparations. All the men whose
names were enrolled knew that they were so,
for no secrecy could be observed in that matter.
Thus by a sort of correlated process the "enlist-
ments" of those who were opposed to the Draft
were perfected and recorded by the officers of
the National Government. In the lower wards
of the city the enrolment made a clean sweep,
and acted as a sort of coercive measure, compel-
ling the mutual union and organization of such
as proposed in any manner either to resist or escape its consequences.

Those who determined to resist organized in
secret, while those who only proposed to escape
formed local clubs of "mutual insurance," among
the membership of which the cost of any required substitute should be divided. This latter
movement was entirely legitimate, and was fos-
tered by patriotic citizens as tending to enhance
the benefit and to diminish any deleterious effects
of the exemption-clause of the Conscription Act.

The more venomous and secret organizations were so successful in concealing their operations, that to the very last their existence was denied by the press until their purposes had passed into performance. That they did exist became then manifest, whether or not they were to any great extent in communication with agents of the Confederate authorities. There was no lack of time, it would seem, for the perfecting of these secret preparations, although much hindrance must have resulted from mutual distrust and fear of betrayal. At the last, however, the fact became apparent that those who prepared to resist were lacking in unity of organism, and they so conducted their operations as to suggest the idea that they had failed to receive an expected leadership and cooperative support. The results of the Gettysburg fight had a great deal to do with the rising of the New York mob in more ways than may appear upon an over-hasty examination.

The sections of the mob could send word to one another and could all rise in the course of one day, but they could not co-operate upon a definite plan after they had risen, simply because they had no such plan. In the general public mind, accustomed to obey the laws and satisfied as to

20

the integral fact that the war must go on and that the army must be supplied in some manner, cost what it might, a sort of apathy had fallen over the whole question. So late as Sunday morning, July 12th, the *New York Daily Times* began its report of the Draft proceedings on Saturday as follows:

"Not until yesterday morning did the majority of the citizens of New York believe that the government was in earnest about the Draft."

Silently and unostentatiously as well as efficiently had the War Department performed the extensive work of enrolment and preparation.

The entire city knew at last that the day for the Draft had been fixed, for it was published in all the morning papers of July 10, 1863. The announcement was accompanied by no great amount of editorial comment, so fully was the public mind supposed to be accustomed and educated to regard the Draft as a surely coming event. The enrolment was well known to have been completed, and the processes of selection were in the iron hands of the National Government.

The enrolment for the city and county of New York embraced somewhat over two hundred thou-

sand names. The required quota of men was between twenty-five thousand and twenty-six thousand, but to this fifty per cent had been added as a
prudent allowance for such drafted men as should
be found exempt from military duty for physical
or other causes. This was a large allowance, in
the view of most men, and accusations of injustice
were freely made.

As thus increased, the Draft called for about
one man in every five of the entire number upon
the lists, and it brought closely to every man who
knew himself to be enrolled the peril in which he
stood of being marched off to future Gettysburgs
and Antietams, or worse. It was announced that
all drafted men would at once be transferred to
Riker's Island, in the harbor, preparatory to being organized, or distributed among existing regiments.

The latter plan was afterwards adopted, and
no regiment in the army could be stigmatized as
"drafted" instead of "volunteer." Under the
provisions of the law, an especial order for the enforcement of the Draft was required to be issued
for each and every Congressional district. (See
Appendix.)

To this, on publication, was added a supplementary order from the Provost-Marshal-General, specifying the sub-districts and other details. Full explanations of the exemption-clause were published by the War Department. (See Appendix.)

Official copies of the regulations made for the Draft were printed in the newspapers of July 11th. On the same day it was announced that the Draft would " begin this morning," in the Twenty-second Ward, forming the Third Subdivision of the Ninth Congressional District. The number of men called for from this sub-district was about twenty-five hundred, including the fifty-per-cent allowance. The marshal's office was at No. 677 Third Avenue, at the corner of Forty-sixth Street, in a neighborhood thickly settled, but not commonly accounted specially unruly. The men who were to make it memorable in the history of the city were to assemble in it from other neighborhoods.

So far, therefore, as the course of events in New York City was concerned, all things had seemed to work together to prepare the requisite apparent " cause" or excitement for the unloosing of its underworld. But, also, a strangely cooperative series of events had prepared an apparently perfect " opportunity," as follows :

The aspect of all military affairs, North and South, had been equally gloomy at the date of the passage of the Conscription Act, but the people of the North had seen only their own side of the great picture. They had no means of obtaining an idea of how much more gloomy and hopeless was the prospect presented to the rulers and people of the crushed and decimated South. As the slow months went by, the news of each succeeding day plainly indicated the approach of a climax. The disasters of the Confederacy in the West were but poorly compensated by its costly victories won in Virginia, and its rulers found themselves under a stern necessity of making some desperate effort to retrieve themselves. They were in constant communication with their sympathizers in the Northern States, and were led, in their fevered and unsound state of mind, to believe the " oppressed masses" of the North ripe for insurrection. It must have been something like insanity, it was certainly a marvellous forgetfulness of all they knew of human nature, which could have induced politicians so able to credit the idea that the farmers and other working-men of the prosperous communities beyond their lines were eager for a transfer of the Civil War and its horrors to their own door-yards. Strange as was the illusion, it is the entire secret of the frantic folly which led to the sending of General Lee to conquer the millions of the North with an army of only ninety thousand men, and that, too, with the Army of the Potomac surely marching upon his flank or thundering upon his rear. All the armies the South could have raised and sent must necessarily have marched to certain ruin; but the Confederate leaders had another expectation than that of mere conquest by the force of their own arms. General Lee was sent across the border with the finest army ever gathered by the Confederacy in order that his movement might act as a summons and his forces serve as a nucleus for all the disaffected elements of the North. It is very probable that the Richmond government had more method in its madness than can now be definitely ascertained. It may have had clearer information concerning, for instance, the purposes of the New York mob leaders than had the press or police of that city. There were Confederate agents everywhere, and

there is room now for little more than surmise as
to what might have followed had Meade's army
been routed at Gettysburg. It is quite likely that
every Northern rifleman would have been in the
ranks in ten days' time, Draft or no Draft ; but the
tides of popular feeling are beyond prophecy or
calculation.

The invasion of the North under General Lee,
therefore, was a political as well as a military undertaking, and a great deal had been done beforehand in many ways to prepare for its success.
It is to be taken for granted that the Confederate authorities believed themselves entitled to
expect an uprising of all elements at the North
which were hostile to emancipation, to war taxes,
to Lincoln, and the Draft. The severe defeat of
Lee at Gettysburg rendered any such uprising on
a large scale out of the question, but it did not
check the fermentation of the elements already
so deeply stirred, nor the operation of the
hidden forces already seething and boiling in the
city of New York. At the same time the presence of a Southern army on Northern soil was
of itself sufficient to quadruple the existing
stock of Unionism in every class and community.

There was an express and peculiar local reason why the movement of General Lee rendered an explosion of the dangerous classes in New York especially possible. Not only were they made to feel the burden of the war, but most of them felt it for the first time. They paid no taxes that they were aware of, and their over-full ranks had not been thinned by any volunteering. The northward movement of the forces under General Lee began early in the month of June, 1863, and was quickly comprehended by the Union commanders. President Lincoln at once called upon the States of New York, West Virginia, Pennsylvania, and Maryland for one hundred and twenty thousand men for temporary service, in view of the extent of the frontier to be watched and guarded and the uncertainty as to the intended movements of Lee's several columns. The Army of the Potomac promptly moved after its old enemy—at first under General Hooker and then under General Meade. The Potomac was crossed by the successive corps of Lee from the 22d to the 24th of June, and the battle of Gettysburg was fought during the first three days of July. Lee was defeated ; but so great was still the uncertainty as to his remaining strength and means of reinforce-

ment that the temporary troops were not re-
leased and sent home for a number of days.

The President's call for one hundred and
twenty thousand men was responded to, for
the greater part, by the already trained and
uniformed militia of the four States named.
This was peculiarly true of the State of New
York, whose National Guard organization was
in excellent condition and well commanded.

No less than seventeen first-rate regiments
went to the front from the cities of New York
and Brooklyn alone, and not one of these returned in time to more than aid in the last clearing of the streets after the power of the mob
was broken.

As the day approached for the completion
of the enrolment and the enforcement of the
Draft, the attention of the President and the
War Department became more and more ab-
sorbed by the rapid course of military events.
All thought was intensely concentrated upon
the movements of the armies in Pennsylvania,
Maryland, Virginia, and in the Mississippi
Valley.

The Confederacy was staggering and reeling
southward under blow after blow. The Gettys-

burg fight had been won, and Lee was stubbornly retreating into Virginia with the wreck of his beaten but indomitable army.

Vicksburg had fallen, and Grant was advancing to the capture of Port Hudson and the final recovery of the Mississippi River to its mouth. The New York militia were turning their camp duties into a sort of midsummer picnic, instead of being ordered home to face the unimagined desperation of the mob in their own streets. The entire North was beginning to draw long breaths of relief. All the more intelligent membership of the disaffected political factions had become thoroughly aware that the day for any open activity of a treasonable nature had gone by, or had failed to arrive. The hallucination of the Richmond government had ended in disaster, and its hope of Northern sedition had melted like mist.

More than commonly, therefore, were all good citizens satisfied as to the probable easy and unobstructed working of all legally authorized operations, and especially of all such as related to the vigorous prosecution of what was now so manifestly a successful war. Less and less grew any foreboding of trouble in the enforcement of the

Conscription Act. The very journals which most bitterly denounced it would have vigorously resented an assertion that they were proposing mob action.

All things had worked together, however, and the 13th of July came to a city whose ripeness for sedition was all the more perilous because the fever of it was supposed to have subsided.

XVI.

Then and Now.

THE story of the great riot of 1863 presents with terrible distinctness the undisputed fact that social volcanic forces continuously exist in great cities. Few men have any idea of their extent and power, or of how completely they are prepared for an eruption.

The city of New York had no more expectation of that outbreak than the city of Charleston had of its recent earthquake, but it is evident that in each case disaster waited only for its hour. The earthquake was beyond human perception, prevention, or control; but these other destructive forces are themselves human, and can be sought out, studied, understood, and held in absolute suppression.

Without unwisely undertaking too wide an inquest, there is yet something to be learned by a further analysis of the Draft Riot and its conditions.

The story of the " Black Joke" firemen has been told, and much of its lesson is obvious. They gave the needed muscular impetus to the first rush of disorder. They expressed an ebullition of wrathful excitement connected with the conscription, and shared by many other men who were not at all evil-minded. Behind them followed the mob, and the " Black Joke" firemen had not so much as thought of that or of the deeds it was about to do. Yet it is a social monster, which must be thought of by all men who are not of it, and who are yet at any time tempted to make a beginning of seditious violence.

What is the mob? What did it consist of in 1863? What might such a thing be made up of now?

It is matter of record that ruling spirits of the mob of 1863 sent agents to the men employed in the iron-works, machine-shops, ship-yards, docks, factories, printing-houses, warehouses, and other gathering places of intelligent working-men, using every argument and menace to obtain recruits. As a rule, the messengers of evil made their appeals in vain. Few, indeed, of the working-men came out and down to commit theft, arson, or murder, while hundreds took up arms as volunteers in defence of all that the mob was assailing. "American working-men" — foreign-born and native-born, uniformed and un-uniformed—did their duty as free men and citizens, and at last fought down and crushed the mob. They were not of it then, and they are not of it now.

This fact, however well ascertained and plainly stated, does but preface another part of the attainable evidence.

Somebody has said that a great city is a great sore; but if New York is the sorest city in the country, it is so because it is the largest gathering of elements which are to be found also in all other municipalities. It has no monopoly of the mob or of mob-probabilities.

In 1863 New York City proper occupied the island of Manhattan, and was bounded on the north by Harlem River and Spuyten Duyvil Creek. The upper part of the city, indicated sufficiently by a line drawn across the island at Fifty-seventh Street, was in many respects different from the older part of the city lying south of that line. This older part was then and is now remarkably cut up into " quarters," larger and smaller, of business interest and of residence and population. Each of these " quarters" has local peculiarities which act as magnets upon all the fast_ arriving human beings. Steamer after steamer brings its living cargo to the Battery. On landing, a large part of each cargo goes West, but all that remains here finds its own place and places as naturally as water runs down-hill.

Race and language are the first potent segregators; yet they do not altogether govern the process, but moral and social conditions, grade by grade, have their peculiar effect. Rascals and land-pirates from London, or Cork, or Paris, or Berlin, or any other European hive, discover their New York communities as if by some secret affiliation. Honest trades are hardly so prone to congregate as are the trades which have but a dim perception of what honesty may be, or consider it a more perfectly developed science of robbery.

Both for good and for evil, therefore, this, like other American cities and some States, contains communities as completely German, Italian, Irish, and so on, with the children born among them, as can be found in Germany, or Italy, or Ireland, or the other countries indicated. And, while the better part of this foreign immigration rapidly takes on citizenship, and becomes self-supporting, self-respecting, law-abiding,—thoroughly "American,"—there is yet another part, of which all Europe is very glad to be relieved, and it is almost sure to prefer city life to any other. The imported sore rarely spreads far into the agricultural districts except during the "tramp" season.

A fair illustration of the tendency to form the race-colonies referred to may be found in the Census reports of the distribution of the colored population in 1860. This was mainly native-born, but the white population generally regarded it as in some manner "foreign," so far as they were concerned. It was thus divided:

1st Ward	111	12th Ward	263
2d "	67	13th "	562
3d	24	14th "	1,075
4th	67	15th "	778
5th '	1,396	16th "	629
6th '	334	17th "	308
7th	141	18th "	404
8th	2,918	19th "	563
9th	424	20th "	1,471
10th	198	21st "	368
11th	225	22d "	146

The colored people in the upper wards were mostly domestic servants, and the collections in the lower wards were swollen greatly beyond these proportions after the Civil War began. The hunters of colored men and women and children during the riot knew only too well where to find them. Whole rows of buildings could be characterized as " negro barracks," and condemned for that reason to be sacked and burned.

The city of New York is, as now constituted, supposed to contain nearly 1,400,000 people. In 1863 the island of Manhattan, then the city, contained 813,669 residents. The neighboring cities on the Long Island and New Jersey shores were peopled by the same races and in about the same proportions. The foreign-born population of New York was 383,345 whites and a few colored, while its native-born whites numbered 383,285, with 12,574 colored natives.

A large part of those recorded as " native-born" were children of foreign-born parents ; for by the same census of 1860 the city contained 280,439 persons under fifteen years of age. It should not be forgotten that the great majority of all immigration consists of male adults.

That part of our foreign-born population which

21

is fit to be free should look at such facts as these, and consider that it has heavy duties relating to the other part.

The immigrated half of the people of New York contained:

Irish	203,740	Scotch	9,208
German	119,984	French	8,074
English	27,082	Italian	1,474

The remainder was divided among other nationalities, and there have been great changes, since that day, in the relative proportions.

By the same census, the State of New York contained, of native-born adults unable to read or write, including those who were of foreign-born parentage, 26,163 persons. Of foreign-born adults unable to read or write there were 95,715. The greater part of this dense ignorance was congregated in or near the city of New York.

During the year ending on June 1, 1860, the total number of persons actually convicted of crime or misdemeanor in the State of New York was 58,067. Of these only 15,230 were native-born, including children of foreign-born parentage, while the foreign-born criminals numbered 42,837. The greater part of these were to be found in the city of New York and its immediate vicinity.

The convicted criminals of the interior and of other States also flowed towards this centre. This is the record of only one year, and that of previous and succeeding years helps greatly in understanding the great riot. The city of New York contained not half so many as now, but still many thousands of foreigners who had been actually convicted of offences against the laws of this country since their arrival. To these add all whose conviction took place somewhere in Europe. Add the large number of unconvicted criminals of both sorts. Held in reserve behind these there was and is the army corps of the very ignorant and degraded, who are not yet actually criminal, but are ripe to become so.

Now draw a broad black line between all of these and our honest fellow-citizens of foreign birth, lest anybody should assert that a "volunteer special" has narrow prejudices. As to another point, the criminal is by nature a drone; and the enforced drudgery performed by any convict out of jail does not entitle him to the honorable name of "working-man."

The immigration since that day has been enor-

mous, and its character is decidedly worse rather
than better. More than that, a whole generation
of toilers and idlers born on the soil, but of un-
Americanized parentage, has grown up in a
mental atmosphere of hungry dissatisfaction.
Hopeful men may say that it is in a state of fermentation needfully preceding its improvement,
but all processes of fermentation suggest supervision and control. Effervescence is well enough,
but explosions are dangerous. Administration
unwarily defective in supervision and control of
a known fermentation permitted the outbreak of
1863. The unwariness then had its more than
ample excuse, which could not be found for any
remissness at the present day.

Repeated utterances of seditious journals and
of criminal demagogues in the United States as
well as in Europe have received ample illustration, here as there, in the evidence produced in
the trials of Dynamiters and Anarchists for felonies actually committed. A tide of testimony
as to this part of the social peril pours unceas-
ingly through the public press, and does not need
to be quoted here. There are features of it, however, which strongly suggest a comparison of the
mob of 1863—undrilled, only partly armed, having

but a vague nucleus of organization, and crazily directed—with the present increasingly-effective aggregate of perverted human nature, asserted by itself and almost judicially assured to be ripening and nearly ready for a blind plunge into Anarchy, which means into the resistless processes by which it must be crushed.

The military aspect of affairs is changed less than many suppose by the awful destructiveness of the dynamite bomb. The hand-grenade is a weapon well studied and understood by military men. Nothing more effective was ever devised for the self-destruction of a tumultuous assembly. It is true that if bomb-throwers in the upper stories of the houses on First Avenue, in July, 1863, had accurately delivered dynamite bombs among the men of Winslow's command or Putnam's, the howitzers or field-pieces would have been alone in a minute of time. Yet it is also true that if the bomb-throwers, with or without instructions, had missed that aim a little and had delivered their bombs a few yards farther north, there would quickly have been no mob there. The bomb is not a handy weapon for street-warfare, as is the locust club; its peculiar powers belong to a line of even more infernal suggestiveness.

The Metropolitan Police of 1863 may have been stronger with reference to the mob then rising than the present Police with reference to such a mob as might now rise. If this be so, the record then made has a peculiar present significance. Not long since, the writer of this book asked of a veteran police official of high rank:

" What, in your opinion, would be the result if to-day another outbreak should come, precisely as that of 1863 came ?"

" In the first place," he said, " no such thing would be allowed to come."

Beyond a doubt that is the received and sound doctrine of the police authorities. He was reminded that concurrent circumstances favored the mob in 1863, and the first question was repeated :

" What if, in spite of all precautions, such an outbreak should actually come ?"

" They might sweep us away like chaff, at first !"

" And the military?" asked the writer.

" No," he said. " Not so. They must be on hand at the beginning."

This means that now as then there would be much bloodshed and devastation before order could be restored. Only a small part of the population of any city is really in favor of a general tumult. There are about thirty thousand known convicts in the city of New York, and it is quite possible that the unknown are as numerous. A large part of all have had no military training whatever. Another large part have served in European military organizations. They are drilled soldiers, as familiar with the use of weapons and at least twice as numerous as are the members of the city regiments of the National Guard militia. An outbreak, once free to attract the depraved and the reckless, would grow and gather strength to-day precisely as in 1863 ; and in like manner be beaten and burn itself out, leaving more or less of wreck and ruin behind it.

The question whether or not sedition could hold the city for any length of time, if asked at all, is answered by the map of Manhattan Island. No matter by what force it might be held, that force could be assailed, simultaneously, from the foot of every street along the entire water-front and from the Westchester mainland. George Washington knew he could not hold the island for a week after the British were ready to move against him, they having naval superiority.

There are yet other semi-military points worth noting. Up and down the long and densely-peopled island runs as a sort of spine the thorough-fare known as Broadway. From this the easterly and westerly streets run towards the water-fronts, and all streets and avenues running north and south have some kind of relation to it, except a few on the extreme east and west.   Near its lower end Broadway and its branches form a cluster of short streets devoted to finance and commerce. Here and below is the very oldest part of the city; and here, marked by Trinity Church, is the real centre of the metropolis, even geographically (though not as to population), due account being taken of the suburbs on the opposite shores of the bordering waters—Brooklyn on the east, Jersey City and Hoboken on the west.   Within easy rifle-shot of Trinity Church are the Custom-house, Sub-Treasury, Stock Exchange and other Exchanges, Trust Companies, the greater banks and banking-houses, the insurance companies, and many large commercial houses, with a multi-tude of minor business interests. ·Within that radius there are riches untold, and all men are well aware that such is the fact.   Gold and silver and jewels and stocks and bonds and vast wealth of costly merchandise are there ready for the hand of the spoiler, if that could by any means be laid upon them. This is the very portion of the city the most easily guarded and defended, while seemingly the most exposed. Forces of any kind can be landed on all the wharves and concentrated on any point named. All the great buildings of stone and brick and iron are so many possible forts. They could be held by small garrisons for days against anything but cannon—and a mob should have no cannon, by any possibility. Look at the Sub-Treasury building for a moment: it is evident that as soon as its doors are closed front and rear, and its window-blinds of hammered steel, with their heavy steel gratings, the place is impregnable to anything short of artillery. A mob might rave around it for weeks if its garrison were well provisioned, and all assailants would be under the practice-fire of safely-concealed marksmen.

Only during a few hours of each day could the Sub-Treasury fall an easy prey to any assault. From 10 o'clock A.M. until 3 o'clock P.M. of all business days the great doors are open wide, and the general public comes and goes at will. Of course the watchful guardians of its interior prevent all unbusiness-like or suspicious lingering within the limits, but there are recurring times when long lines of clerks and others are standing before the gratings of the receiving and disbursing desks, waiting their turns to be served. Among these might be easily marched in a hundred armed conspirators, awaiting the signal for a concerted attack, sure to be successful if boldly made and accurately supplemented by the arrival of exterior support and co-operation. The "fort" with its contents would be in the hands of a well-ordered and skilfully conducted mob in ten minutes from the hour agreed upon. If the Custom-house should be captured at the same hour, with a few other central buildings, Broad and Wall and Nassau streets and lower Broadway would be under the range of their windows, the tables would be turned, and nothing short of artillery (or siege and starvation) could readily dislodge the mob. The real protection of this district, therefore, as of the entire city, rests in providing any such possible banditti with an abiding assurance that in case of their "success" the artillery would be there within the hour. Something like that idea stands guard now; for the forts on Governor's Island are in full view from the Battery, and there are always armed vessels in the harbor. Still, it would do no harm if the idea were materially strengthened in some sufficiently public manner to prevent its ever being overlooked, and to avoid the damages of retaking. Before noon of the first day of the riots of 1863 a mountain howitzer, full to the lips with grape and canister, scowled down the stone steps of the Custom-house, while a hundred suddenly-enlisted citizens occupied the front of the Sub-Treasury, ready to go inside as a garrison if required. The greed of the mob for other plunder, the imperfection of their plans and organization, and the promptness with which protective measures were taken saved the financial district.

The temptations to an anti-property mob eager to obtain property are all there now, but all the new buildings are better adapted than were the old to be turned into forts for that side of any conflict which might first garrison them.

With purely social questions and reformatory measures this book has nothing to do, but it cannot close without stating convictions which are the result of thoughtful investigation.

The working-men are now, as in 1863, the community's real bulwark against disorder. The mob will helplessly grind its teeth in its den so long as it finds that intelligent labor is more and more clearly aware that upon its own head and heart must fall the worst part of the disasters involved in even partial and temporary anarchy.

The lessons of the riot of 1863 should never be lost sight of by the working-men, whose predecessors not only refused to join in its infernal rush, but helped to put it down.

In the minds of the mob itself must also be erected another barrier against outbreak, and one not less important than the first, in a full and steadily-maintained conviction that every riot will be *crushed at its very beginning.*

The evil-disposed must have a consciousness of the perpetual presence of abundant power in capable and unhesitating hands. To this must be added an assurance of searching, uncompromising, unforgetting justice at the hands of judges and juries.

After a most minute examination, it seems plain that no blame for the riot of 1863 attaches to the United States Government, or to the State government, or to the municipal or police authorities. It may be well, however, for men now or hereafter intrusted with the guardianship of the public peace to consider that if by a momentary weakness any official shall elect that a thousand shall die instead of half a dozen, his indignant fellow-citizens will lay at his door the blood of every man, woman, and child who perishes by reason of his fault. All men know that there is and always will be a volcano under the city, but they are justly sure that there is no need of an eruption.

Weakness, timidity, or time-serving compliance with lawlessness in any form provokes attack; sturdy insistence on order, and ready strength, are the only safety.

APPENDIX.

I.—POLICE.

IT is not easy to do justice to the Metropolitan Police of the city of New York in the year 1863. Never before or since has any similar body of men been in better condition for duty. They were carefully and well selected. The rank and file were sober, self-respecting, self-reliant, thoroughly drilled and equipped, and they were admirably organized and commanded. They had perfect confidence in their leaders, and the leaders had unbounded confidence in the discipline, courage, and devotion to duty of the men. The resulting *esprit de corps* was remarkably strong. The Metropolitans as a body believed themselves fully competent to deal with any possible rising of the disorderly forces with which they were accustomed to deal. Under ordinary circumstances they were undoubtedly able to justify their self-confidence, but the great riot compelled them to face extraordinary circumstances. How they faced them is of itself deserving a lasting record. At the same time it is not just to them or to others to form a false or exaggerated idea of their numerical strength, or a diminished idea of the power with which they contended, or a false estimate of their actual performances.

The following is a synopsis of the last quarterly report of Superintendent Kennedy before the riot: Superintendent, 1 ; inspectors, 4; clerks, 8 ; surgeons, 5; captains, 41 ;

sergeants, 159; roundsmen, 64; patrolmen, 1620; special
duty, 109; special duty out of precinct, 165; special duty
of a sanitary nature, 37; acting as janitors, etc., 84; total,
2297.

The general scope of police operations in each precinct
can better be understood by noting the precise locality of
its headquarters, or "station-house." These were at
that date as follows :

POLICE HEADQUARTERS,

300 Mulberry Street, near Bleecker Street.

First Precinct..........29 Broad Street, near Exchange Pl.
Second Precinct.........49 Beekman Street, near William St.
Third Precinct.........160 Chambers St., near Greenwich St.
Fourth Precinct.........9 Oak Street near Chestnut Street.
Fifth Precinct..........49 Leonard St., near W. Broadway.
Sixth Precinct ....9 Franklin Street, near Baxter St.
Seventh Precinct........247 Madison Street, near Clinton St.
Eighth Precinct.........127 Wooster Street, near Prince St.
Ninth Precinct..... ...94 Charles Street, near Bleecker St.
Tenth Precinct.........Essex Market.
Eleventh Precinct.......Union Market.
Twelfth Precinct.......126th Street, near Harlem River.
Thirteenth Precinct .....178 Delancey St., near Attorney St.
Fourteenth Precinct.....53 Spring Street, near Mulberry St.
Fifteenth Precinct.......221 Mercer Street, near Bleecker St.
Sixteenth Precinct.......156 West 20th Street, near 7th Ave.
Seventeenth Precinct....Corner 1st Avenue and 5th Street.
Eighteenth Precinct......163 East 22d Street, near 3d Ave.
Nineteenth Precinct.....East 59th Street, near 3d Avenue.
Twentieth Precinct......352 West 35th Street, near 9th Ave.
Twenty-first Precinct....120 East 35th St., near Lexington Ave.
Twenty-second Precinct.47th St., between 8th and 9th aves.
Twenty-third Precinct...East 86th Street, near 5th Avenue.
Twenty-fourth Precinct..Steamboat No. 1.
Twenty-fifth Precinct....300 Mulberry St., near Bleecker St.
Twenty-sixth Precinct...City Hall.

Twenty-seventh Precinct . . 117 Cedar St., near Greenwich St.
Twenty-eighth Precinct. . . . 550 Greenwich St., near Charlton St.
Twenty-ninth Precinct. . . . . East 29th Street, near 4th Avenue.
Thirtieth Precinct. . . . . 131st Street, Manhattanville.
Thirty-first Precinct. . . . . . . 86th Street, Bloomingdale Road.
Thirty-second Precinct. . . . . Fort Washington.

During the riots the services of the several captains and other officers were largely performed outside of their respective precincts. Any attempt to do them individual justice of praise would surely result in absolute injustices of omissions. No such attempt has therefore been made.

Of the patrolmen, 1452 were on duty in New York and 168 in Brooklyn, and a mere squad on Staten Island. Since policemen are human, and must eat and rest like other men, not more than half of the force can be on duty at one time, except under the pressure of sudden emergencies. At the moment of the outbreak of the riot, therefore, the city was guarded by less than a thousand policemen, scattered among thirty-two station-houses and over all the long miles of its streets and avenues. It was not until afternoon of the first day of the riot that any large force of them could be gathered to act as one body. The difficulties attending such an aggregation form one of the most noticeable features of the situation. Besides these, the police had within call only its own "reserves" of men off duty, and the as yet uncertain, unascertainable resources of the fragmentary military organizations. What these were it was to discover to its delight and astonishment. It should be borne in mind that whatever were the services rendered by the military forces of every name and nature, and by citizens in any manner volunteering, all these acted and operated as auxiliaries of the police, and were as parts of one body of "preservers of the peace" whereof the Metropolitans were the nucleus.

22

The varying numbers of those who from first to last were engaged in the mob in its many segments and movements cannot so much as be intelligently guessed at. Whatever they were, they were largely augmented in effectiveness by numberless rumors, false alarms, exaggerations, fears, and excitements. It required the coolest and most courageous good sense to avoid panic on the one hand or hasty and futile activities on the other, and to strike hard blows promptly at the right *times* and in the best *spots.*

The police knew nothing of the state of preparation or the plans of their antagonists, and could at first but guess at the real extent and meaning of the public disaster. Other men's hearts all over the city fainted and failed them for fear and astonishment; but not so—not for one moment—did the hearts of the Police authorities and the devoted Metropolitans. Robbed of the services of Superintendent Kennedy on the first morning of the riot, the President of the Board of Police Commissioners was left almost alone. The duties of the Superintendent fell upon him by law. His colleague, General Brown, was on his way to join the army in the field. Commissioner John G. Bergen was compelled to devote himself entirely to the affairs of Brooklyn and other outlying districts and interests. The unnatural field of battle in New York City was left under the sole management of Thomas C. Acton, and from Monday morning at six o'clock until Friday morning he did not sleep nor change his clothing. With extraordinary fortitude and endurance he stood at his post during every successive hour of day and night until the struggle was over, and the victory had been definitely won for law and order.

Almost the entire field of actual rioting was within the more densely peopled part of the island city. The police headquarters, commonly spoken of as "The Central Office," on Mulberry Street, between Houston and Bleecker streets, was centrally located, and in direct telegraphic communication wtih all police station-houses, and with many other prominent points and public buildings in the city and vicinity.

General Harvey Brown, commanding the United States troops in the city, placed himself and his men entirely at the disposal of President Acton. He became, personally, part of the Central Office garrison. Under the efficient management of Seth C. Hawley, Chief Clerk of the Police Department, its commissariat quickly attained efficient system and large proportions. His ordinary duties were such as called for special ability and industry. He was now compelled to add to them the care and provision for the men on duty, and for swarms of helpless negroes in all parts of the city. They fled to all the police-stations from the pursuit of their destroyers. Not less than eight hundred of them reached the Central Office building. The aged, the sick, the blind, the lame, the women and the little ones, came pouring in, and Mr. Hawley dealt kindly with them all. Nevertheless, this fact rendered the Central Office more than ever an object of mob-bitterness, and increased the peril of an attack upon it. On the third day of the riot General Brown noticed that President Acton's face was clouded a little. He did not ask the reason then, and when he •did so afterwards he did but learn what was well known to him at the time : Every soldier was in the field, and so was the police force, beyond any message of recall ; the building, with its eight hundred helpless fugitives, was garrisoned only by General Brown, Mr. Acton, Mr. Hawley, and ten tired-out policemen, and there was imminent danger of an attack. The building could not have been held for a minute, and the general would have been safer on any other battle-field he had ever seen.

Such incidental risks could not be avoided. It was at

no time possible that all the forces operating against the mob, rising on every side like mushrooms, should be controlled, directed, or even perfectly advised, by Mr. Acton. General Sandford, General Brown, and General Wool labored under similar difficulties. Mutual conferences between leaders, or even between leaders and their own immediate subordinates, were by no means easily obtained during the first two days of the riot. Co-operation had to be secured as best it might, amid the heat and hurry and frantic rush of kaleidoscopic emergencies. That it was obtained at all bears witness to a high degree of common-sense among the official personages concerned, and also to the tremendous pressure under which they were compelled to act. Dire necessity was upon all that they should struggle for one common purpose and should stand or fall together. Under such circumstances it was greatly for the public advantage that the many subordinate officers who were forced to act promptly on their own responsibility were to so large an extent men of capacity and of much military or police experience. They were compelled by the action of the mob itself, in many cases, to take measures without waiting for higher authority than the extreme law of self-preservation. They performed a large amount of courageous and well-timed service whereof no record whatever has been preserved, save in oral tradition or individual memories.

II.—THE MILITARY.

By 6 o'clock P.M. of Monday, July 13th, there were a thousand officers and soldiers gathered and registered at the Thirty-fifth Street Armory, besides the rallies at other places unrecorded. On Friday morning the following commands were in actual service in the city :

152d   Reg. New York State Volunteers.
52d   "   "   "   "   "
11th   "   "   "   "   "
13th   "   "   "   "   "   (Cavalry, of Rochester.)
54th   "   "   "   "   "
83d   "   "   "   "   "
26th   "   Michigan   "   "
7th   "   N. Y. State Militia, N. G.
7th   "   "   "   "   "   (Old Guard.)
10th   "   "   "   "   "
74th   "   "   "   "   "
69th   "   "   "   "   "
65th   "   "   "   "   "   (Buffalo.)

(No regimental reports of strength attainable.)

U. S. Sailors and Marines = 700.
     "   Regular Infantry, the garrisons of the harbor forti-
fications, daawn uon daily to keep detachment of
150 in the city.

The praise bestowed by General Brown (see page 350)
upon the troops under his immediate command was equally deserved by a large part of the volunteers and militia,
for they fought well. The men who garrisoned arsenals
and other important places are also to be honored for
bravely and unselfishly coming forward at the call of duty.

III.—THE DRAFT ACT.

The Conscription Act took into account the fact that
the United States contained many Congressional districts
in which it could not be enforced. Others had furnished
their entire quota of men under the law ; and among such
as had not there were wide variations, and justice required special count and care. For each district, therefore, a separate " Proclamation" was issued, of which the
following is a specimen:

" WAR DEPARTMENT, PROVOST-MARSHAL-GENERAL'S OFFICE.
WASHINGTON, D. C., July, 1863.

"*To the Board of Enrolment, Eighth District of New York :*

" In accordance with section six of the Enrolment Act, approved March 3, 1863, I [General Ferry] hereby communicate orders, as follows, from the President of the United States, in reference to calling out the National forces, viz. :

" ' I, Abraham Lincoln, President of the United States of America, and Commander-in-chief of the Army and Navy thereof, having taken into consideration the number of volunteers and militia furnished by and from the several States, including the State of New York, and the period of service of said volunteers and militia, since the commencement of the present Rebellion, in order to equalize the numbers among the districts of the said States, and having considered and allowed for the number already furnished as aforesaid, and the time of their service aforesaid, hereby ordain four thousand, eight hundred and ninety-two as first proportional part of the quota of troops to be forwarded by the Eighth District of the State of New York under this the first call made by me on the State of New York, under the act approved March 3, 1863, entitled "An Act for enrolling and calling out the national forces, and for other purposes;" and in pursuance of the act aforesaid, I order that a draft be made in the said Eighth District for the State of New York, for the number of men herein assigned to said District, and fifty per cent in addition.

" ' In witness whereof I have hereunto set my hand and caused the seal of the United States to be affixed.

" ' Done at the City of Washington, this —— day of July, in the year of Our Lord One thousand eight hundred and sixty-three, and of the Independence of the United States the Eighty-eighth.

" ' ABRAHAM LINCOLN.' "

What was known as " The Rich Man's Exemption" clause of the Conscription Act, and of which so much political use was made, was as follows :

" Section 13. And be it further enacted : That any person drafted and notified to appear, as aforesaid, may, on or before the day fixed for his appearance, furnish an acceptable substitute to take his place in the draft; or he may pay to such person as the Secretary of War may authorize to receive it, such sum, not exceeding three hundred dollars, as the Secretary of War may determine, for the procuring of such substitute, which sum shall be fixed at a uniform rate by a general order made at the time of ordering a draft for any State or Territory; and thereupon such person so furnishing the substitute or paying the money shall be discharged from further liability under the draft. And any person failing to report after due service of notice as herein provided, without furnishing a substitute or paying the required sum therefor, shall be deemed a deserter, and shall be arrested by the Provost-Marshal and sent to the nearest military post for trial by court-martial, unless, upon proper showing that he is not liable to do military duty, the Board of Enrolment shall release him from the draft."

The War Office in Washington had been besieged with applications for information as to legal and other questions connected with operations under the Conscription Act, and had taken great pains to answer them. The following is a quotation from Circular No. 44, issued on the 12th of July and published in New York on the 14th, signed by the Provost-Marshal-General :

" To answer the inquiries made to this office, it is announced:

" 1. Any drafted person paying three hundred dollars. under section 13 of the Enrolment Act, is thereby exempt from liability under that draft, but not from any subsequent draft.

" 2· Any drafted man furnishing an acceptable substitute is exempt from military service for the period for which said substitute is mustered into the service."

Notice was duly given that the general draft would begin upon Monday, July 13th, but that in some of the more perfectly prepared sub-districts it would commence upon Saturday, the 11th.

IV.—PROCLAMATIONS.

The first proclamation by Governor Seymour, dated July 14, 1863, was printed and circulated on the 15th. It was as follows :

"PROCLAMATION BY GOVERNOR SEYMOUR.

" TO THE PEOPLE OF THE CITY OF NEW YORK: A riotous demonstration in your city, originating in opposition to the conscription of soldiers for the military service of the United States, has swelled into vast proportions, directing its fury against the lives and property of peaceful citizens. I know that many of those who have participated in these proceedings would not have allowed themselves to be carried to such extremes of violence and of wrong except under an apprehension of inJustice; but such persons are reminded that the only opposition to the conscription which can be allowed is an appeal to the courts. The right of every citizen to make such an appeal will be maintained, and the decision of the courts must be respected and obeyed by rulers and people alike. No other course is consistent with the maintenance of the laws, the peace and order of the city, and the safety of its inhabitants. Riotous proceedings must and shall be put down. The laws of the State of New York must be enforced, its peace and order maintained, and the lives and property of all its citizens protected at every hazard.

" The rights of every citizen will be properly guarded and defended by the Chief Magistrate of the State.

" I do therefore call upon all persons engaged in these riotous proceedings to retire to their homes and employments, declaring to them that unless they do so at once I shall use all the power necessary to restore the peace and order of the city.

" I also call upon all well-disposed persons, not enrolled for the preservation of order, to pursue their ordinary avocations. Let all citizens stand firmly by the constituted authorities, sustaining law and order in the city, and ready to answer any such demand as circumstances may render necessary for me to make upon their services; and they may rely upon a rigid enforcement of the laws of the State against all who violate them.

"HORATIO SEYMOUR, Governor."

In immediate connection with the Governor's proclamation was generally published the following

" NOTICE.

NOTICE FOR THE PURPOSE OF PERFECTING A CITIZENS' OR-
GANIZATION.

" All citizens are requested to assemble immediately at the following places, when they will be enrolled under the direction of the persons hereinafter named, viz.:

"City Assembly Rooms: Gen. Ward B. Burnett.

"Seventh Regiment Armory: Gen. Abram Duryea, Maj. S. R. Pinckney, Capt. John W. Avery.

"Central Market Drill-rooms: Col. John D. MacGregor, Chas. G. Cornell, Capt. John D. Ottiwell.

"Room north-east corner of Thirty-second Street and Broadway: Col. J. Mansfield Davis, Capt. R. Smedberg, Fourteenth Regiment U. S. A.

"City Hall: Col. Robert H. Shannon, Captain T. Rynders, Capt. T. S. Murphy.

"No. 220 Third Street: Capt. H. Sewer, F. Repper.

"By order of

"HORATIO SEYMOUR, Governor.
"JOSIAH T. MILLER, Inspector-General."

The second proclamation issued by Governor Seymour also bore the date of July 14th, but was first published in the morning papers of Friday, the 16th. It was as follows:

"PROCLAMATION.

" *Whereas*, It is manifest that combinations for forcible re-sistance to the laws of the State of New York and the execution of civil and criminal process exist in the city and county of New York, whereby the peace and safety of the city and the lives and property of its inhabitants are endangered; and

" *Whereas*, The power of the said city and county has been exerted, and is not sufficient to enable the officers of the said city and county to maintain the laws of the State and execute the legal process of its officers; and

" *Whereas*, Application has been made to me by the Sheriff of the city and county of New York to declare the said city and county to be in a state of insurrection:

"Now, therefore, I, Horatio Seymour, Governor of the State of New York and Commander-in-chief of the forces of the same, do, in its name and by its authority, issue this proc-lamation, in accordance with the statute in such cases made and provided, and do hereby declare the city and county of New York to be in a state of insurrection; and give notice to all persons that the means provided by the laws of this State for the maintenance of law and order will be employed to whatever degree may be necessary, and that all persons who shall, after the publication of this proclamation, ' resist, or aid in resisting, any force ordered out by the Governor to quell or suppress such insurrection ' will render themselves liable to the penalties prescribed by law.

" Horatio Seymour.

"New York, July 14, 1863."

The Mayor's first public utterance related to arms and ammunition, viz.:

"PROCLAMATION BY THE MAYOR.

"MAYOR'S OFFICE, NEW YORK,
July 14, 1863.

"It is highly important to the peace of the city and the suppression of the existing riot that the rioters shall not be allowed to furnish themselves with arms and ammunition; and I do hereby accordingly enjoin upon all persons who keep arms and ammunition for sale that they will at once cease selling to private persons and close their places of business.

"GEORGE OPDYKE, *Mayor.*"

The first note of encouragement uttered by Mayor Opdyke was as follows:

"PROCLAMATION BY THE MAYOR.

"MAYOR'S OFFICE, NEW YORK,
July 15, 1863.

"TO THE CITIZENS OF NEW YORK: I am happy to announce to you that the riot which for two days has disgraced our city has been in good measure subjected to the control of the public authorities.

"It would not have interrupted your peace for a day but for the temporary absence of all our organized militia. What now remains of the mob are fragments, prowling around for plunder; and for the purpose of meeting these and saving the military and police from the exhaustion of continued movements, you are invited to form voluntary organizations, under competent leaders, to patrol and guard your various districts. With these exceptions you are again requested to resume your accustomed daily avocations. This is necessary to your personal security as to the peace of the city.

"The various lines of omnibuses, railways, and telegraphs must be put in full operation immediately. Adequate military protection against their further interruption will be furnished on application to the military authorities of the State.

"Fellow-citizens, the laws must and shall be obeyed; public

order shall not be broken with impunity. Our first duty now is to restore the public peace and preserve it unbroken, and to pursue and punish the offenders against the majesty of the laws.

"GEORGE OPDYKE, Mayor."

V.—ARCHBISHOP HUGHES.

The daily morning papers of Thursday, July 16th, contained the following :

"AN APPEAL TO THE IRISH CATHOLICS FROM ARCHBISHOP HUGHES.

"In the present disturbed state of the city I will appeal not only to them, but to all persons who love God and revere the holy Catholic religion which they profess, to respect also the laws of man and the peace of society, to retire to their homes with as little delay as possible, and disconnect themselves from the seemingly deliberate attempt to disturb the peace and social rights of the citizens of New York. If they are Catholics, or of such of them as are Catholics, I ask, for God's sake, for the sake of their holy religion, for my sake, if they have any respect for the episcopal authority, to dissolve their association with reckless men who have little regard for Divine or human law.

"✠ JOHN, Archbishop of New York."

As a better method of reaching any who might ac knowledge his authority or influence, he also issued the following pastoral letter, which appeared as a "poster" all over the city, early on Thursday morning :

" *Archbishop Hughes to the Men of New York who are now
called in many of the Papers Rioters :*

" MEN : I am not able, owing to rheumatism in my limbs,
to visit you, but that is not a reason why you should not
pay me a visit in your whole strength.   Come, then, to-morrow, Friday, at two o'clock, to my residence, north-west corner of Madison Avenue and Thirty-sixth Street.   I shall have
a speech prepared for you.   There is abundant space for the
meeting around my house: I can address you from the corner
of the balcony.   If I should be unable to stand during the
delivery you will permit me to address you sitting.   My voice
is much stronger than my limbs.   I take upon myself the responsibility of assuring you that in paying me this visit, or
in retiring from it, you shall not be disturbed by any exhibi-
tion of municipal or military presence.   You who are Catholics, or as many of you as are, have a right to visit your
Bishop without molestation.

"✠ JOHN HUGHES, *Archbishop of New York.*"

VI.—MILITARY ORDERS.

During the entire week the papers of New York and
Brooklyn teemed with the rallying notices and orders of
many commanders of the fragmentary volunteer and
militia forces.   The reproduction of these is needless.
Successive "reliefs" of the Regular Army detachments
on duty in the city had enabled large parts of the garrisons of the harbor forts to take their turns in street-fighting.   On the morning of Friday, July 17th, General
Harvey Brown was relieved by General E. R. S. Canby,
and issued and published the following:

" ORDERS : In obedience to instructions from the Secretary of War, the undersigned relinquishes the command of the United States troops in the city and harbor of New York.

" In parting from the troops of his command in the harbor he desires to express his sense of their uniformly good and soldierly conduct, and he cannot separate from those of his immediate command in the city without his testimony of their bravery, discipline, and soldierly deportment.

" Engaged night and day in constant conflict with the mob, they have in some fifteen or twenty severe contests, in most of them outnumbered ten to one,—many of the mob being armed, —whipped and effectually dispersed them, and have been uniformly successful.

He paid a general complimentary tribute to the soldiers, especially commending Lieutenant-Colonel John B. Frothingham, Adjutant-General upon his own staff. He added :

" Having, during the present insurrection, been in immediate and constant co-operation with it, he desires the privilege of expressing his unbounded admiration of the Police Department of this city. Never, in civil or military life, has he seen such untiring devotion and such efficient service.

" To President Acton and to Commissioner Bergen he offers his thanks for their courtesy to him and their kindness to his command.

HARVEY BROWN, *Brigadier-General*."

SOUTHERN CALIFORNIA:

ITS VALLEYS, HILLS AND STREAMS; ITS ANIMALS, BIRDS AND FISHES; ITS GARDENS, FARMS AND CLIMATE.

BY THEO. S. VAN DYKE,

Author of " The Still Hunter," " The Rifle, Rod and Gun in California," etc.

12mo Extra Cloth, beveled, - - - - $1.50

In this book, as the author tells us, he treats of *home.* After long years of residence in Southern California,—not in its cities and seaports, but in its mountains and valleys and by its streams, camping, hunting, and studying the country, he now sends forth this book as the record of his experience and knowledge. It describes fairly and honestly all the advantages and disadvantages of Southern California for the settler, the farmer, the invalid, the climate-hunter, the fruit-raiser, the sportsman, the fisherman and the traveler.

"It is the best work on the subject that we have ever seen."—*Rochester Union and Advertiser.*

"The most truthful and interesting book on the subject we have yet seen. . . On the last-named subject (sports) the author is no mean authority, and his descriptions of fishing, shooting and camping cannot fail to awaken the sportsman's enthusiasm."—*New York Sun.*

"A variety of topics are presented, some of interest to the pleasure seekers, others to those who would find in Southern California means of livelihood or health. We have yet to read any book wherein a more careful and thorough résumé is presented of the climate of Southern California, a question so vital to invalids. . . Very beautifully does the author describe the sequence of the seasons in Southern California and the flowers which sing of these gradual changes.—*New York Times.*

"Is without question the best book which has been written on the Southern Counties of California. . . We think that any reader will recognize his truthfulness and fairness. . . . . . . We omit all mention of the entertaining chapters on the Sports and the game of Southern California. Anyone who has dipped into Mr. Van Dyke's previous books will know what to expect when he descants on his specialty. . May be commended without any of the usual reservations."—*San Francisco Chronicle.*

"His impartiality and thoroughness are manifest from the first, and a great deal of valuable information is told in an entertaining manner. . . It has not a dull page in it.--*Visalia* (Cal.) *Delta.*

"Unlike most of the emanations of the press concerning this state, it is not overdrawn."—*San Buenaventura* (Cal.) *Press.*

"The result is a book in which the ideas and impressions of a true lover of nature and a facile and graceful writer are expressed with sincerity and candor."—*Boston Literary World.*

"The book does not bear the stamp of an immigration document, designed to attract settlers to a particular locality, but seems to have been written with a desire to tell to those who are interested *the whole truth, and nothing but the truth,* about Southern California."—*Buffalo Express.*

"Mr. Van Dyke is an old resident of California, and his powers of observation and ability to picture graphically what he has seen were acknowledged by all who read his book "The Still Hunter.""—*Phila. Record.*

"He is an accurate and charming writer and impresses one as having had experience amid the scenes he describes. . . It should and doubtless will have a large circulation."—*Utica Press.*